Test your
Business
Vocabulary
in Use

George Bethell
Tricia Aspinall

CAMBRIDGE
UNIVERSITY PRESS

PUBLISHED BY THE PRESS SYNDICATE OF THE UNIVERSITY OF CAMBRIDGE
The Pitt Building, Trumpington Street, Cambridge, United Kingdom

CAMBRIDGE UNIVERSITY PRESS
The Edinburgh Building, Cambridge CB2 2RU, UK
40 West 20th Street, New York, NY 10011–4211, USA
477 Williamstown Road, Port Melbourne, VIC 3207, Australia
Ruiz de Alarcón 13, 28014 Madrid, Spain
Dock House, The Waterfront, Cape Town 8001, South Africa

http://www.cambridge.org

First published 2003
Reprinted 2003

Printed in Italy by G. Canale & C. S.p.A.

Typeface Sabon 10/12pt   *System* QuarkXPress® [KAMAE]

A catalogue record for this book is available from the British Library

ISBN 0 521 53254 X

Contents

Introduction

What is in this book?

This book is designed to help you test the vocabulary you have learnt through studying *Business Vocabulary in Use* by Bill Mascull. It contains 66 unit tests – one for each unit of the *Business Vocabulary in Use* book. Each test is closely matched to the content of the relevant study unit. You will find the Answer key at the back of the book.

There are also four summary tests. These occur after every 16 or so units. Use these to check your progress. There are answers and guides to interpreting the scores you achieve in the summary tests.

How do I use the unit tests?

There are five stages in preparing for and using the tests.

- **Preparation:** Study a business vocabulary unit thoroughly. When you feel confident that you have mastered *all* the key words, you are ready to do the relevant test.
- **Testing:** Each test includes a variety of tasks – matching words to their meanings, selecting the right word from a number of alternatives, writing words to complete sentences, etc. Each question tests one important piece of vocabulary. Try to do all the questions in the test.
- **Marking:** When you have finished all the tasks, check your work. Then use the Answer key at the back of the book to mark your test. Give yourself one mark for a completely correct answer and zero for an incorrect answer. Add up all your marks to get your total score.
- **Interpreting your score:** Compare your total score with the target score for the test. (You will find this at the top of the test.) If you reach the target score you can feel confident that you have learnt most of the important vocabulary for the unit.
- **Revision:** If you do not reach the target score, you probably need to do more work. Go back and revise the unit. Use your test results to find the words you did not know and the sections where you were weak. Concentrate on learning these.

How long do the tests take?

The unit tests are not timed. Each one will probably take between 10 and 15 minutes, but take as long as you need to get the highest mark possible. The summary tests are longer and are likely to take about 45 minutes to complete.

We hope that these tests will support you while you improve your business English and that they will help you to master the important vocabulary that you will need in your work. We also hope you will enjoy using them and achieving high scores.

George Bethell and Tricia Aspinall

Work and jobs

1.1
6 marks

Use a word from the box to complete each sentence. The first one is an example.
There is one extra word that you don't have to use.

0 I ....*work*.......... for Morgans the aircraft company.
1 I .... the manufacturing plant in Cambridge.
2 I am in charge .... the production team.
3 About 120 people work .... me.
4 Coordination between production and design is my ....
5 I .... with a lot of people in the company and with our customers.
6 I'm .... for a budget of over € 100 million.

deal
responsible
~~work~~
job
manage
under
of
responsibility

1.2
6 marks

Decide whether each statement is about full-time (FT), part-time (PT), permanent (P)
or temporary (T) work. Tick the right box. The first one is an example.

	FT	PT	P	T
0 I work from 9 to 5 during the week and 8 to 12 on a Saturday.	✓			
1 I joined the company ten years ago and I guess I'll be here for another ten.				
2 I do four hours each morning and then I pick the children up from school.				
3 I've been here since March and I'll leave in July when the designs are finished.				
4 We are supposed to work $37\frac{1}{2}$ hours a week but I usually do a bit more.				
5 I started here when I left school. Oh, that's about 20 years ago now.				
6 This job is only for six months, but that's OK because then I'm going to Italy.				

1.3
6 marks

Write one word from the box below in each gap to complete the text.
The first one is an example. You may choose to use some words more than once.

at	for	in	of	off	on	get	to

'My name is Anne Scott and I work ....*for*....... a public relations company in London. I leave
.... work at 7 o'clock in the morning. I go .... work by train and I usually
.... to work by 8.30. I'm always .... work till about 6 o'clock so I never get
home before 7.30 pm. Last year I broke my leg and so I was .... work for over a month.
I didn't like being at home. I love my job. I would hate to be permanently out .... work.'

1.4
4 marks

In each sentence, write the correct form of the word given in brackets ( ).
The first one is an example.

0 I'm responsible for .....*managing*..... the design team.   (manage)
1 I'm in charge of .... the work of the team.   (coordinate)
2 One of my responsibilities is to .... sure that we don't spend too much money.
                                                                                     (make)
3 My team is responsible for the .... of new models for production.   (design)
4 I'm in charge of .... our work for the whole year.   (plan)

2.1
6 marks

Draw a line from each word on the left to a word on the right to make a word pair. (There is one extra word that you don't have to use.) The first one is an example.

physically	contact
human	work
problem	on
day	demanding
team	commute
clock	shift
working	solving
	hours

2.2
6 marks

Decide whether each statement is about regular office work (OW), teleworking (TW) or shift work (SW). Tick the right box. The first one is an example.

	OW	TW	SW
0 I'm at work by 8.30 and I leave for home at 5 o'clock.	✓		
1 I work from 10 at night till 6 in the morning for four weeks, then I switch to days.			
2 We turned one of the bedrooms into an office and that's where I do all my work.			
3 When I'm working nights, it's really difficult to sleep during the day.			
4 Some people find the 9-to-5 routine boring, but I like working with other people.			
5 I clock in at 8.55 every day and I'm at my desk till 5 pm.			
6 The difficult thing is that my home is my office so I'm there 24 hours a day.			

2.3
6 marks

Choose the best word from the brackets ( ) to fill the gap. The first one is an example.

0 I had a 9-to-5 ....job.......... when I left school but I hated it.   (job/work)
1 We have a .... system, but everyone must be here between 10 and 2.
                                                              (repetitive/flexitime)
2 I work from .... and simply send my work over the Internet.   (house/home)
3 I just sit in front of a computer all day, but this work is mentally ....
                                                              (tiring/routine)
4 This is the most .... job I've ever had. There is never a boring minute.
                                                              (stimulating/repetitive)
5 We all look forward to 5.30 because then we can .... off for the day.   (shift/clock)
6 The 7.30 train to London is always full of ....   (commuters/telecommuters)

2.4
6 marks

For each word, write one word which means the *opposite*. The first two or three letters are given. The first one is an example.

0 mentally   p h y s i c a l l y
1 easy   h a _ _   4 dull   e x _ _ _ _ _ _
2 interesting b o _ _ _ _   5 unstimulating f a s _ _ _ _ _ _ _
3 varied   r o u _ _ _ _   6 undemanding   t o _ _ _

Recruitment and selection

3.1
4 marks

Draw a line from each word on the left to a word on the right to make a word pair. (There is one extra word that you don't have to use.) The first one is an example.

covering	agency
employment	references
application	test
curriculum	letter
psychometric	form
	vitae

3.2
7 marks

Choose the best word from the brackets ( ) to fill the gap. The first one is an example.

0 We need to ......*recruit*...... four new people for our office in Manchester.   (join/recruit)
1 We are using a recruitment .... to find them for us.   (agency/headhunter)
2 They advertised the .... in the local newspaper last week.   (positions/applicants)
3 So far, over 60 people have applied for the ....   (works/posts)
4 We are going to look at all the letters of .... over the weekend.
(application/situation)
5 On Monday, we will draw up a .... of 10 or 11 people.   (reference/shortlist)
6 Then we'll invite them all to come for an ....   (interview/appointment)
7 We hope to .... the successful applicants by the end of the month.   (apply/appoint)

3.3
6 marks

Look at each sentence. Would you find it in the Situations Vacant section of a newspaper (SV), in an applicant's CV, or in a covering letter (CL)? Tick the right box. The first one is an example.

	SV	CV	CL
0 'The post offers a starting salary of £17,000 plus benefits.'	✓		
1 'I enclose my résumé for your consideration.'			
2 '1997–2000 University of Maryland, MBA (Marketing and Public Relations).'			
3 'I am looking for a more stimulating environment and your company offers this.'			
4 'Training will be given but basic word-processing skills would be an advantage.'			
5 '1994–1997: The Biscuit Company, London – Manager responsible for 22 staff.'			
6 'The successful applicant will be expected to take up the post in January.'			

3.4
6 marks

Find a word related to each clue. Some of the letters are given.

1 Certificates from school and university
2 Where you've worked and what you've achieved
3 Hire a good person who is working for another company
4 People you can contact to find out about an applicant
5 Process to find the right person for a job
6 An applicant who has a good chance of getting the job

1	q				f				t				s
2	e	x											
3	h				u								
4	r		f										
5	s				c			n					
6	c		d		d								

Skills and qualifications

4.1
6 marks

Write one word from the box below in each gap to complete the text. You may choose to use some words more than once. The first one is an example.

| with | from | in | as | for | at |

'My name is Jean Wilson and I have just started working ....*in*.......... a bank. I graduated .... Edinburgh University last year with a degree .... Business and Management. Now I am going to train .... an accountant. I think I will do well because I am good .... figures and I am skilled .... using computers. I think that training .... a specific job will be more interesting than the general education I got at university.'

4.2
6 marks

Choose the best word from the brackets ( ) to fill the gap. The first one is an example.

0 Everyone should stay in full-time ....*education*..... until they are at least 18.   (school/education)
1 Of course .... qualifications are important, but they're not everything.
                                                            (printed/paper)
2 I look for people with lots of relevant .... experience.   (job/work)
3 Our company runs some very good in-house .... courses.   (training/skilled)
4 Last year we spent over £50,000 on management ....   (experience/development)
5 We value people who are highly .... and want to get on.   (motivated/graduated)
6 Tom gets on well with everyone. He is a great team ....   (person/player)

4.3
6 marks

Look at these sentences taken from job advertisements. Are they describing work which is highly skilled (HS), skilled (Sk), semi-skilled (S-S), or unskilled (U)? Tick the right box. The first one is an example.

	HS	Sk	S-S	U
0 'Experience of managing a modern production plant is essential.'		✓		
1 'Wanted – Early morning cleaners for office block in the centre of town.'				
2 'Eastern Buses now recruiting drivers. Competitive salary plus benefits.'				
3 'Building labourers required. Good money for hard workers.'				
4 'Pilot with experience of flying 747s required for new cargo carrier.'				
5 'Local electrical company requires production line workers now.'				
6 'Black Box Games needs an experienced software developer. Good salary.'				

4.4
6 marks

Find a word related to each clue. Some of the letters are given.

1 Good at working on his/her own
2 Works in a systematic, orderly way
3 Good with figures
4 Naturally very good at what they do
5 Someone who is good with PCs is 'computer-...............'
6 Works well on his/her own

1	p	r	o				
2	m	e	t	h			
3	n	u	m				
4	t	a	l				
5	l	i	t				
6	s	e	l	f	-	d	

Your score
/24

5.1
7 marks

Choose the best word from the brackets ( ) to fill the gap.

1 I work in a small hotel in Amsterdam. I .... €8 an hour.   (earn/paid)
2 It's not a lot, but it's more than the .... wage.   (maximum/minimum)
3 Some customers leave me .... and that is a great help.   (perks/tips)
4 My sister works in a bank and her .... is €3,000 a month.   (salary/wages)
5 The bank also provides her with a good .... package.   (bonus/benefits)
6 Next year she thinks she will get a .... car.   (company/business)
7 When she is 55 she will be able to give up work and live on her ....
(package/pension)

5.2
7 marks

**Read the job advertisements. Write one word in each gap to complete the sentences.
The first letter of each word is given. The first one is an example.**

0 In this job, the _wages_ are £224 for 37 hours.
1 The p........................ is just over £6 an hour.
2 Workers get £10 an hour for any o........................
   they do.
3 There are some p........................ including
   free meals.
4 This job offers a b........................ salary
   of £1000 a month.
5 You get 10% c........................ on
   everything you sell.
6 When you sell enough you get a
   b........................ of £400.
7 There are some f........................ benefits
   including a pension.

> **Production Line Workers**
> £224 for a 37-hour week (£6.05 per hour).
> £10 an hour for any additional hours.
> Benefits include a company pension scheme and
> free meals in our new canteen.
> For further details, phone Paul on 020 8843 6060

> **JOIN OUR SALES TEAM**
> WE OFFER £1,000 PER MONTH PLUS 10% OF ANY SALES YOU
> MAKE. AND, IF YOU MEET YOUR MONTHLY SALES TARGET, WE GIVE
> YOU AN EXTRA £400.
> WHAT ELSE? WELL, THERE'S A COMPANY PENSION SCHEME AND AN
> ALLOWANCE OF 40P PER MILE WHEN YOU USE YOUR OWN CAR.
> IF YOU WANT THESE REWARDS, CALL 020 8844 8800.

5.3
6 marks

**Match each statement with a word or phrase from the list below. Write the letter of your chosen
answer next to the statement. (There is one extra word/phrase that you don't have to use.)
The first one is an example.**

0 American term for all the benefits that an employee receives.	C
1 Payment for those who have stopped working – especially due to age.	
2 Benefit that lets employees buy company shares at a low price.	
3 This describes bonuses given for reaching objectives set by the company.	
4 Money paid to an employee who is asked to leave an organization.	
5 Formal word for all the pay that an employee receives.	
6 Director of a company who is paid a huge salary . . . but doesn't deserve it.	

Your score
/20

A severance payment   B stock options   C compensation package   D remuneration
E performance-related   F fat cat   G boardroom row   H pension

6.1
6 marks

Draw a line from each word on the left to a word on the right to make a word pair.
(There is one extra word that you don't have to use.) The first one is an example.

support — collar
technical — support
shop — force
open — office
head — staff
blue — union
work — floor
— plan

6.2
8 marks

Choose the best word from the brackets ( ) to fill the gap.

1 The CEO is the head of the .... team.   (administration/management/organization)
2 We have 200 people on our ....   (recruitment/business/payroll)
3 Our .... department is responsible for recruitment.   (personnel/employee/worker)
4 Our main office is in London but we have .... all over the country.
(places/companies/sites)
5 I supervise all the .... workers on the production line.
(manual/white-collar/labour)
6 I am in charge of training in the human .... department.   (support/resources/staff)
7 We have a .... of 65 in London and about 30 in Paris.   (staff/union/headquarters)
8 You haven't been paid this month? OK, I'll put you through to the .... department.
(pay/salary/finance)

6.3
6 marks

Write one word in each gap to complete the conversation. The first letter of each word is given.
The first one is an example.

'Fellow workers, I'm calling for a _walk-out_ .... because the company says that it will not
increase our pay by more than 2% this year. That is not good enough so we must take
i........................... action now. All workers who are in the u........................... should stop work
immediately.'

'I don't agree. If there is a s........................... we won't get paid. We should refuse to work more
than 35 hours a week. An o........................... ban would make management listen to us.'

'That won't be enough. We should also stage a g...........-s........... . If we don't work very quickly,
the company will lose money. Then they'll talk to us.'

'Right, then. Do we all agree?'

Your score
/20

The career ladder

7.1
7 marks

Match each statement with a word from the list below. Write the letter of your chosen answer next to the statement. (There is one extra word that you don't have to use.) The first one is an example.

0 We used to have four layers of management but now we have only two.	B
1 I am an independent software designer. At the moment, I'm working for three companies.	
2 I don't know whether my job here is safe. I could be out of work next month.	
3 In 1999 we had 430 employees. Now there are only 280.	
4 We used to do our printing in-house, but now it's done by a company in Hong Kong.	
5 I was a shop floor supervisor but then they made me manager of the whole production plant.	
6 Our company has been completely reorganized to make it more efficient.	
7 Now that we have reduced our costs, we are making much more money.	

A downsize   B delayer   C restructure   D outsource   E promotion
F freelance   G dismiss   H profit   I insecurity

7.2
10 marks

Choose the best word from the brackets ( ) to fill the gap.

1 I didn't like the way the company was being run so I ....
(resigned/sacked/terminated)
2 They laid .... 200 people in March and 50 more in September.   (on/off/out)
3 I joined this company because the career .... is excellent.   (path/way/contract)
4 I have regular performance .... with my manager.   (advice/support/reviews)
5 We now have fewer employees and so the company is much ....
(efficient/leaner/fatter)
6 I have worked my way up and now I am a .... manager.   (main/old/senior)
7 She was .... for copying company software on to her PC.   (fired/promoted/retired)
8 I was appointed on a .... contract so my job isn't very safe.
(permanent/full-time/temporary)
9 When you join a company now you can't expect a .... for life.
(job/work/career)
10 If you break the safety rules you can be .... immediately.
(downsized/dismissed/delayered)

7.3
7 marks

Write one word in each gap to complete the conversation. The first three letters of each word are given. The first one is an example.

'We have to restructure..... our company if we are to survive. We will have a fla.............. structure with only two levels of management. We don't want to make anyone red.................... . Some of our senior people will take early ret................... . The rest will be offered posts, but they may be at a lower level. No one likes to be dem................ but it is better than being out of work. We hope people will be fle.................... and move to different jobs. If anyone decides to hand in their not................ we will help by offering out.................. advice. This is a very difficult time for us all.'

8.1
6 marks

The symbols represent possible problems at work. Match each statement (1–6) with the right symbol. Write the letter of your chosen answer in the box on the right. You may use each symbol more than once.

A	B	C	D	E	F

1 That bottle of acid should be locked in the store room. If it gets on your skin it will burn you.	
2 Only two people smoke in our office, but even that makes it difficult for me to breathe.	
3 This safety guard MUST be in place at all times. Anyone who removes a guard will be sacked.	
4 Last winter it got so cold that we all had to go home until the heating was fixed.	
5 I've got a pain in my fingers and wrists. It must be due to all that data entry we did last month.	
6 Caution! This machine must only be used by a trained operator.	

8.2
6 marks

Choose the best word from the brackets ( ) to fill the gap.

1 I've cut my finger. Can you get the .... aid kit for me?   (health/injury/first)
2 That pile of waste paper is a fire ....   (precaution/hazard/exit)
3 This special keyboard reduces the risk of repetitive .... injury.   (strain/stress/stroke)
4 There is no smoking here because of the dangers of .... smoking.
                                      (passive/passionate/personal)
5 I reported the missing fire extinguisher to the health and .... inspector.
                                      (danger/hazards/safety)
6 The poor air-conditioning system makes it a bad working ....
                                      (environment/place/zone)

8.3
8 marks

In each sentence, there is *one* word which is *wrong*. Circle the mistake and write the correct word at the end of the line. The first one is an example.

0 All companies should have a dignity at work (police.)   ....*policy*........
1 My last manager was a terrible bull. He shouted at us all the time.   ....
2 Finally, he was sacked for sexual harass because of his remarks to women.   ....
3 The judge said the company had discriminated about Mary Chambers.   ....
4 There was a wooden ceiling which prevented her from being promoted.   ....
5 This was obviously a case of serious woman discrimination.   ....
6 The company said it had an equal opportune policy but I don't believe it.   ....
7 I was the only black employee and I was a victim of racism discrimination.   ....
8 We need some affirmative activation here like they have in America.   ....

Your score
/20

Managers, executives and directors

9.1
8 marks

The diagram below shows the management structure of Universal Software. Match the people (1–8) with their positions. Write the letter of your chosen answer in the box on the right.

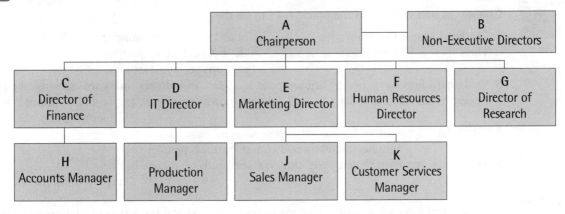

1 I'm Marco Alatri and I'm the director responsible for the company budgets and accounts.	
2 I'm Tom Scott. I'm not actually a manager at Universal, but I do sit on the board.	
3 My name is Helen Good. I'm the CEO and I also chair the board.	
4 My name's Carla Jelinek. I'm in charge of the company's information systems.	
5 I'm Dan Matthews. My team develops new products and tests them.	
6 I'm Karine and my team deals with calls from the public . . . and complaints!	
7 I'm Alex Tait and I'm responsible for company recruitment and staff development.	
8 My name is Patrick Aubaile and I report to the CFO.	

9.2
6 marks

Choose the best word from the brackets ( ) to fill the gap.

1 Our sales manager heads .... a department of 40 people. (out/off/up)
2 I work in accounts and Tina is my .... manager. (line/head/over)
3 I work for Franz and I think he is the best .... I've ever had. (boss/executive/director)
4 I was in .... management for 10 years before I became a director. (medium/middle/vice)
5 Tanya Minelli is .... Marketing at Global Foods in New York. (VP/COO/CFO)
6 She's the only woman here who has a .... executive position. (higher/chief/senior)

9.3
4 marks

Find a word related to each clue. The first letter is given in each case.

1 Where company directors hold their meetings
2 Head of a company in the US
3 What 'F' stands for in CFO
4 Another term for the chief executive: Managing ....

1	b						
2	p						
3	F						
4	D						

Business people and business leaders

10.1
6 marks

Choose the best word from the brackets ( ) to fill the gap.

1 The Ford Motor Company was .... in 1903.   (find/found/founded)
2 There were 2,700 business .... in the UK in the last quarter.
(start-ups/get-ups/start-offs)
3 Sir Richard Branson is one of Britain's .... of industry.   (bosses/captains/moguls)
4 Rupert Murdoch is a media .... who owns many newspaper and TV companies.
(leader/magnate/founder)
5 That's Angelina Carlito. She's a very successful ....
(businessman/businesswoman/business people)
6 My mother started with one shop and now she heads up a huge business ....
(empire/country/world)

10.2
6 marks

Write one word in each gap to complete this text. The first and last letters of each word are given.

'My name is John Forbes. I'm 29 years old and I've just started my fourth company. I guess I am
an e _ _ _ _ _ _ _ _ _ _ r because I am good at e _ _ _ _ _ _ _ _ _ g new businesses. My aim is
to g _ _ w a new company until it is big enough to survive and develop. Then I move on. I like
taking risks so just managing an organization would be too boring. To tell the truth, I don't have
the l _ _ _ _ _ _ _ _ p skills necessary. I can't see myself as a software t _ _ _ _ n like Bill Gates.
I just want to make the most of the e _ _ _ _ _ _ _ _ _ _ _ _ l skills that I do have.'

10.3
7 marks

Find the answer to each clue. One or two letters are given in each case.

1 Woman or man who has their own company
2 Owns film studios – perhaps in Hollywood
  (2 words)
3 One who started a company
4 Collective term for TV, radio, newspapers
5 Owns wells and pipelines – for 'black gold'
  (2 words)

1	b						p			
2	m					m				
3	f									
4	m									
5	o			m						

11.1
6 marks

Draw a line from each word on the left to a word on the right to make a word pair.
(There is one extra word that you don't have to use.) The first one is an example.

big
corporate
self
e-
free
enterprise
nationalized

industry
commerce
employed
business
enterprise
department
profits
zone

11.2
6 marks

Choose the best word to fill each gap from the alternatives given below. Put a circle around
the letter, A, B or C, of the word you choose.

'The economy of eastern Europe has changed a lot. Twenty years ago, the main industries were
completely nationalized and many companies were owned by the (1) .... They did not
work well. They were inefficient and (2) .... Now governments are trying to (3) ....
them, but it is not easy to find (4) .... People don't want to put money into the old
companies. However, some people are happy to (5) .... their money on new businesses
and there are signs that a new enterprise (6) .... is growing.'

1 A nation	B state	C country
2 A automatic	B diplomatic	C bureaucratic
3 A privatize	B nationalize	C enterprise
4 A corporations	B firms	C investors
5 A save	B risk	C sell
6 A culture	B commerce	C concern

11.3
8 marks

Decide what each statement is about. Write the missing word. (The first letter is given.)

1 'We use our initials "TFT" inside a blue arrow. It's on all our notepaper.' *corporate* l _ _ _

2 'It was a bad idea. We lost a fortune and the company collapsed.' *commercial* d _ _ _ _ _ _ _

3 'We're based in the US but we operate in over 30 countries.'

m _ _ _ _ _ _ _ _ _ _ _ *corporation*

4 'We specialize in helping SMEs.' *small or medium* e _ _ _ _ _ _ _ _ _ _

5 'We want people to see us as expensive – but offering the very best quality.'

corporate i _ _ _ _ _

6 'We meet once a month and we aim to help local businesses.' c _ _ _ _ _ _ *of commerce*

7 'By next year, all our business will take place on the Internet.' *electronic* c _ _ _ _ _ _ _

8 'I was a manager, but I'm working my way up and I hope to be a director soon.'

corporate l _ _ _ _ _

Your score
/20

12.1
6 marks

Write the missing word in each sentence.

1 I work for myself. I have been s _ _ _ - employed for ten years.

2 We borrowed £80,000 from the building s _ _ _ _ _ _ to buy our house.

3 We became a p _ _ _ _ _ limited company last year and since then our share price has risen by 15%.

4 I work for myself so the tax office classifies me as a s _ _ _ trader.

5 We are a not-for-p _ _ _ _ _ organization dedicated to providing health services for the poor.

6 Like lots of charities, we employ a professional to organize our f _ _ _ - raising activities.

12.2
6 marks

Choose the best word to fill each gap from the alternatives given below. Put a circle around the letter, A, B or C, of the word you choose.

Aberdeen Reliance is one of the country's smaller life insurance companies. It was set up in 1920 as a (1) .... This means that the 15,000 people who have insurance policies with the company are (2) .... These, in theory, own all the (3) .... and there are no (4) .... Last year, the board of directors wanted to sell the company to a large American (5) .... , but first they had to get the policy holders to agree to (6) .... This was heavily defeated, proving that many people still value the traditional status of the company.

1 A mutual   B public   C incorporated
2 A partners   B directors   C members
3 A profits   B salaries   C expenses
4 A customers   B traders   C shareholders
5 A corporation   B sector   C proprietor
6 A freelancing   B demutualization   C limiting

12.3
6 marks

Find the answer to each clue. The first and last letters are given in each case.

1 Ltd written in full
2 What the 'C' stands for in PLC
3 Someone who works for him/herself – not for one company
4 Organization owned and run by two or more people
5 Charities are in this sector of the economy
6 Money given to a charity

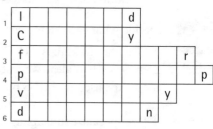

Manufacturing and services

13.1
7 marks

Match *each* picture with one of the industries listed in the table. Write the letter of the picture next to the right industry. Some industries may match more than one picture. The first one is an example.

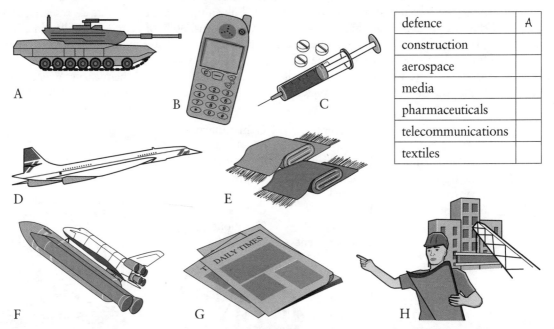

defence	A
construction	
aerospace	
media	
pharmaceuticals	
telecommunications	
textiles	

A   B   C   D   E   F   G   H

13.2
6 marks

Match each statement with one of the service industries listed in the box. There is one extra industry that you don't have to use. The first one is an example.

| catering   financial services   healthcare   leisure   property |
| retail   telecommunications   tourism |

0 In our shop we sell high quality shoes from Italy. .... *retail* ....
1 We offer low-cost package holidays in Spain, Portugal and France. ....
2 We manage the largest, and most modern, private hospital in England. ....
3 We have 22 executive flats to sell close to the city's business district. ....
4 We currently supply in-flight meals to seven international airlines. ....
5 Our health and sports clubs can be found in over 130 hotels in the UK. ....
6 We give advice on how to save money or where to invest it. ....

13.3
6 marks

Choose the best word from the brackets ( ) to fill each gap.

1 I spent 25 years in the US, working in the .... industry.   (automobile/automobiles)
2 In Britain, shipbuilding and other .... industries found it hard to survive in the 80s.
(light/heavy)
3 Telecommunications was one of the .... industries of the 1990s.   (growing/growth)
4 We don't build computers: we just write the ....   (software/hardware)
5 We manufacture refrigerators, washing machines and other household ....
(goods/parts)

Your score
/19

6 Biotechnology is the new, ... industry of the 21st century.   (processing/emerging)

The development process

14.1
8 marks

Choose the best word to fill each gap from the alternatives given below. Put a circle around the letter, A, B or C, of the word you choose.

'We are very excited about our new multimedia range. The original (1) .... was to produce a large, flat screen that would hang on the wall like a picture. Our (2) .... research showed us that people don't want huge TVs in their living rooms. 80% of people who filled in our (3) .... said they wanted one screen to be a TV, a computer monitor, or used to show DVDs. It took us two years to make the (4) .... When we showed it to our (5) .... group, they loved it. There were one or two small (6) .... , but we solved them easily. We are having a big product (7) .... next week and our sales (8) .... is approximately 100,000 units in the first year.'

1 A design   B concept   C manufacture
2 A market   B shop   C laboratory
3 A application   B interview   C questionnaire
4 A trial   B version   C prototype
5 A focus   B panel   C thought
6 A insects   B bugs   C flies
7 A launch   B survey   C rollout
8 A team   B department   C forecast

14.2
6 marks

Choose the best word from the brackets ( ) to fill the gap.

1 We did a .... in which we interviewed 200 members of the public.
(survey/research)
2 I am on the .... panel for Smiths Frozen Meals.   (researcher/consumer)
3 We hope to produce this medicine on an industrial .... by 2006.   (size/scale)
4 Our new drug is .... against all common forms of malaria.   (effective/active)
5 In .... , 90% preferred the taste of our new coffee.   (trials/questionnaires)
6 We'll see what customers think of the new model after the .... in April.
(rollout/forecast)

14.3
6 marks

Find a word related to each clue. The first letters of the answers are given.

1 Another word meaning 'idea'
2 The final test version
3 IT system used for design and manufacture
4 Another word for a 'fault'
5 Where scientists develop new drugs
6 Ask people to return faulty products

1	c						
2	b						
3	C						
4	d						
5	l						
6	r						

Your score
/20

15.1
6 marks

Fill the gap in each sentence by writing the correct form of the verb given in brackets. The first one is an example.

0 Suzanne King is in charge of product ...*development*... at Westworld Electronics.   (develop)
1 I want to be a graphic .... when I graduate.   (design)
2 I think that the Internet is the greatest .... of the past 50 years.   (innovate)
3 We are looking for someone with .... of databases and spreadsheets.   (know)
4 Christopher Cockerell was the .... of the hovercraft.   (invent)
5 You have to pay a lot to get a good software ....   (develop)
6 Have you seen her .... for the new shopping centre?   (design)

15.2
10 marks

Draw a line from each word on the left to a word on the right to make a word pair. (There is one extra word that you don't have to use.) Then use your word pairs to complete the sentences below. The first one is an example.

patent	development
product	licence
cutting	property
research	application
under	copyright
intellectual	centre
	edge

0 We have made a ....*patent application*........ to stop people copying our invention.
1 Our drug for pain relief is made .... in 32 countries.
2 I'm in charge of .... at Minnow Technologies.
3 We use the latest technologies to keep our products at the ....
4 We took them to court because the original idea was our ....
5 We test all new drugs at our .... in Zurich.

15.3
6 marks

Choose the best word from the brackets ( ) to fill the gap.

1 I bought a PC just five years ago and now it is ....   (innovative/obsolete)
2 Our new engine uses state-of-the-........................... electronics.   (art/science)
3 I think that the .... of computer control systems is fascinating.
                        (technology/knowledge)
4 Advanced, ... systems are great, but there is more to go wrong.
                        (low-tech/hi-tech)
5 I receive a .... of 10% on all my books that the publisher sells.   (royalty/licence)
6 Finding out how antibiotics work was a tremendous ....
                        (breakthrough/breakout)

Your score
/22

16.1
6 marks

Choose the best word from the brackets ( ) to fill the gap.

1 You can buy fresh vegetables and other agricultural .... in the market.
(produce/production)

2 We are the largest .... of printing machinery in the UK.
(manufacturer/manufacturing)

3 Their cars are cheap because they .... them out in huge numbers. (craft/churn)

4 I started working on the production .... ten years ago. (plant/line)

5 There aren't enough skilled workers in the building industry and the .... is getting worse.   (shortage/surplus)

6 .... is a problem in the holiday industry with too many hotels and not enough tourists.   (Overproduction/Overcapacity)

16.2
6 marks

Choose the best word or phrase to fill each gap from the alternatives given below. Put a circle around the letter, A, B or C, of the answer you choose.

'This is where we produce plastic pipes and fittings for the construction industry. This (1) .... was opened in 2001. Everything is highly (2) .... with computers controlling all the machines. The system was expensive to buy but it is very (3) .... When we are working at (4) .... capacity, we can produce 200 kilometres of pipe a day. We only employ 20 people in our (5) .... team so our (6) .... is very high.'

1	A shop	B plant	C works
2	A automatic	B autocratic	C automated
3	A cost-effective	B labour-intensive	C mass-produced
4	A full	B excess	C spare
5	A making	B producing	C manufacturing
6	A intensity	B productivity	C capacity

16.3
6 marks

Find the answer to each clue. Some letters are given to help you.

1 Too much of something on the market
2 Machine that does the work of a human
3 Place where goods are made
4 Where parts are put together to make a product: .... line
5 Where a craftsman makes, for example, pieces of furniture
6 Not produced by a machine but crafted by a person

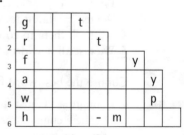

Read the questions carefully. Try to answer them all. This test takes about 45 minutes.

1
10 marks

For each sentence, choose the best word to fill the gap from the alternatives given.
Put a circle around the letter, A, B or C, of the word you choose.

1 This company was set up as a small family .... in 1977.
   A empire   B corporation   C business
2 Sally Green is on the board of ....
   A directors   B founders   C managers
3 Tom East is the .... executive in charge of Marketing.
   A chief   B head   C senior
4 Last year we made .... of £1.5 million.
   A liabilities   B profits   C finances
5 The corporate .... we try to present is of a business that truly values its customers.
   A image   B logo   C ladder
6 We .... about 20 people in our London office and most have been with us
   for years.
   A hire   B employ   C appoint
7 Each year, we .... two or three graduates as trainee managers.
   A recruit   B qualify   C situate
8 We pay reasonable salaries and offer excellent fringe ....
   A perks   B tips   C benefits
9 Next month we are going to .... two new products.
   A forecast   B innovate   C launch
10 We have carried out a lot of market .... over the past year.
   A focus   B research   C development

2
10 marks

Write the abbreviations below in words. One word has been given in each case to help you.

1 HR   H _ _ _ _   Resources
2 IT   I _ _ _ _ _ _ _ _ _ _   Technology
3 CEO   Chief E _ _ _ _ _ _ _ _   O _ _ _ _ _ _
4 CAD   C _ _ _ _ _ _ _   Assisted D _ _ _ _ _
5 RSI   Repetitive S _ _ _ _ _   I _ _ _ _ _
6 PLC   P _ _ _ _ _   L _ _ _ _ _ _   Company

3
5 marks

Match each sentence beginning (1–5) with the correct ending. Write the letter (a–f) of the ending
you choose in the box below. There is one extra ending that you don't have to use.

1	The company has an equal opportunities	a	I was offered early retirement.
2	Please send your application form,	b	with a covering letter, by Monday 9th May.
3	The health and safety inspector noticed	c	policy to fight discrimination.
4	Last month, I achieved my sales target	d	candidates had to do psychometric tests.
5	When the firm downsized,	e	that the fire extinguisher was missing.
		f	so I got a performance-related bonus.

Answers	1	2	3	4	5 ....

4

5 marks

The notice below shows where various departments can be found in the head office of Global Foods PLC. For each statement, decide which floor is needed. Then write the number in the box.

GLOBAL FOODS PLC

Floor 1: Reception

Floor 2: Finance and Accounts

Floor 3: IT

Floor 4: R & D

Floor 5: Marketing and Sales

Floor 6: HR

Floor 7: CEO and Boardroom

	Floor
'The Internet connection has been down for two hours and I want to know what's happening.'	
'Where do I go for the Directors' meeting?'	
'I need the report on the trials of our new range of frozen vegetables.'	
'I want to ask Sarah about the recruitment drive and the training programme for new employees.'	
'My salary wasn't paid into my bank yesterday and I need to speak to someone about it.'	

5

7 marks

Choose one word from the box to complete each sentence. There is one extra word that you don't have to use.

in	out	off	on	as	over	against	for

1 Daniel has applied .... a job as a software designer.
2 I start work at 8.30 and I clock .... at 5 pm.
3 Mary was discriminated .... because she is a woman.
4 Tanya is very skilled .... using PCs.
5 George works .... the production line at Ford.
6 There are currently 780,000 people .... of work in the UK.
7 I trained .... a teacher but now I sell luxury cars.

6

8 marks

Complete the tables by writing in the British or American English equivalents of the words given.

	American	British
1	stock options	_ _ _ _ _ options
2	automobile industry	_ _ _ industry
3	labor union	_ _ _ _ _ union
4	flextime	_ _ _ _ _ _ _ _

	British	American
5	property	real _ _ _ _ _ _
6	CV	_ _ _ _ _ _
7	school leaver	high school _ _ _ _ _ _ _ _
8	sole trader	sole _ _ _ _ _

Draw a line from each word on the left to a word on the right to make a word pair. (There is one extra word that you don't have to use.) Then use your word pairs to complete the sentences below. The first one is an example.

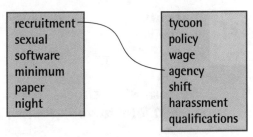

recruitment	tycoon
sexual	policy
software	wage
minimum	agency
paper	shift
night	harassment
	qualifications

0 We used a ....*recruitment agency*........ to advertise for graduates to train as managers.

1 Many healthcare workers are paid the ....

2 I don't have any .... but I've got lots of work experience.

3 I want to be a .... like Bill Gates by the time I'm 25.

4 When he was accused of .... he resigned immediately.

5 I don't like working the .... because I can't sleep during the day.

Complete the sentences below by writing one word in each gap.

1 We set up a focus _ _ _ _ _ to discuss our ideas for a new range of hair care products.

2 We discovered a design _ _ _ _ _ so we had to recall all the cars sold in May and June.

3 I really wanted to work for a charity, but wages are very low in the voluntary _ _ _ _ _ _ .

4 Our sales _ _ _ _ _ _ _ _ for next year is that business will grow by 5%.

5 The designs are our intellectual _ _ _ _ _ _ _ _ and they are protected by patents.

6 When we are working at full _ _ _ _ _ _ _ _ we can produce 22,000 units per hour.

7 I found this job in the situations _ _ _ _ _ _ pages of my local newspaper.

8 I left the company in 1990 and I've been self-_ _ _ _ _ _ _ _ ever since.

In each sentence, there is *one* word which is *wrong*. Circle the mistake and write the correct word at the end of the line. The first one is an example.

0 When the CEO was arrested, our corporate (picture) was severely damaged. ....*image*.........

1 The railways were owned by the state, but they were privately in 1984. ....

2 I believe the strongest economies are built on free entrepreneur. ....

3 Paul has worked in the aerospace industrial for over 20 years. ....

4 Making high quality furniture by hand is very labour-expensive. ....

5 Our CADCAM system is at the cutting side of technology. ....

6 She is training to be a commerce artist in New York. ....

Match each headline to a statement. Write the number of the statement you choose in the box next to the headline. (There is one statement that you do not have to use.)

Fat cats get more ☐

Board faces demutualization fury ☐

Northern Enterprise Zone opens ☐

Western Steel shock: 500 jobs to go ☐

Skills shortage hits construction targets ☐

Rail overtime ban to cause travel chaos ☐

1 Members of Saxon National turned out in force today to vote against the controversial proposal to change the status of one of England's oldest building societies.
2 Trained people are starting to come into the industry but there aren't enough of them and they have little on-site experience.
3 The idea is to attract businesses to the area by offering low commercial taxes and by lifting many of the legal restrictions on the import and export of goods.
4 Union spokesperson Harry Evans said that many of his members wanted a total stoppage but this action would send a strong message to the employers.
5 Liberty Homes PLC announced annual profits of £1.1 million yesterday – an increase of 2.2% on the previous year.
6 Workers, who on Monday were offered 1.2%, were furious to learn that directors had voted themselves a huge 11.6%.
7 Restructuring was necessary to save the plant but the scale of the redundancies came as a terrible blow to the workforce.

> This is the end of Summary Test 1.
> Use the Answer key at the back of the book to check your answers.

Materials and suppliers

17.1
5 marks

Choose the best word or phrase to fill each gap from the alternatives given below. Put a circle around the letter, A, B or C, of the answer you choose.

'We sell parts to more than 100 computer companies. In fact, we are the largest (1) .... of electronic (2) .... in the country. We hold huge (3) .... worth millions of pounds in our (4) .... in Manchester and Southampton. The big manufacturers use us because we provide a just- (5) .... service. They order the parts when they need them and we deliver within 24 hours.'

1	A business	B supplier	C industry
2	A components	B pieces	C bits
3	A stocks	B goods	C works
4	A headquarters	B plants	C warehouses
5	A in-house	B in-time	C in-case

17.2
7 marks

Match each statement to a word or phrase from the list. Write the letter of your chosen answer next to the statement. The first one is an example.

A raw material   B subcontracting   C capital   D finished goods
E labour   F work-in-progress   G in-house   H knowledge

0 We also have a small printing department where we print all our own stationery.	G
1 The steel that we use to make the engines comes from Poland.	
2 We borrowed £20,000 from the bank to cover start-up costs.	
3 At any moment there are about 200 cars on the production line.	
4 We don't have our own drivers – we pay a local company to deliver to our customers.	
5 The most important input is the ideas that come from our R & D department.	
6 We are lucky that we have good managers and a well-trained workforce.	
7 Last week, 2,500 TVs went out of this factory and into the shops.	

17.3
6 marks

Find the answer to each clue. Some letters have been given to help you.

1 To move stocks from one place to another
2 Materials, capital, and labour are all ....
3 Another word for 'paid for'
4 Buy in services from an outside supplier
5 'Lean production' means to make things ....
6 What 'stocks' are called in the US

1	h		d						
2	i	p							
3	f			c	d				
4	o		s		c				
5	e	f					l	y	
6	i	v		t	r		s		

18.1
10 marks

Draw a line from each word on the left to a word on the right to make a word pair. (There is one extra word that you don't have to use.) Then use your word pairs to complete the sentences below. The first one is an example.

continuous	defects
quality	improvement
mystery	practice
zero	control
spot	performance
best	shoppers
	checks

0 We regularly upgrade our products because we believe in ...*continuous improvement*... .
1 To test customer service in our stores we send in ....
2 We look around the industry for examples of .... and then copy them.
3 I believe that .... is all about checking that products match the specs.
4 We can't afford any mistakes. Our target is to have ....
5 We make frequent .... throughout the manufacturing process.

18.2
6 marks

Choose the best word to fill each gap from the alternatives given below. Put a circle around the letter, A, B or C, of the answer you choose.

'I'm Sue Carter, production manager at F1 Parts PLC. We make engine parts for high performance cars. Here we believe in (1) .... quality management. The (2) .... of each part are given to one-hundredth of a millimetre. At every stage we check that our products (3) .... to the specs. We try to get it right (4) .... time because, if there is a defect, (5) .... is very expensive. We are always looking for ways to improve quality and so our motto is (6) .... , which comes from Japanese.'

1 A all	B full	C total
2 A dimensions	B pieces	C components
3 A work	B conform	C exact
4 A one	B first	C last
5 A reworking	B repairing	C recalling
6 A aikido	B bonsai	C kaizen

18.3
6 marks

Write the abbreviations in words.

1 TQM T _ _ _ _   Q _ _ _ _ _ _   M _ _ _ _ _ _ _ _ _
2 BPR B _ _ _ _ _ _ _   P _ _ _ _ _ _   R _ - _ _ _ _ _ _ _ _ _

19.1
6 marks

Choose the best word from the brackets ( ) to fill each gap.

1 Our .... includes several multinational companies. (clientele/economy)
2 We wanted to buy the house but the .... was asking for £300,000.
(purchaser/vendor)
3 The government brought in several market .... to strengthen the economy.
(reforms/pressures)
4 Until 1998, the government fixed all the prices, but now we have a .... market.
(free/state)
5 It's only a small shop, but we serve nearly 200 .... a day. (consumers/customers)
6 Most of our .... are small businesses. (markets/users)

19.2
10 marks

Draw a line from each word on the left to a word on the right to make a word pair. (There is one extra word that you don't have to use.) Then use your word pairs to complete the sentences below.

| customer |
| end |
| street |
| purchasing |
| market |

| users |
| manager |
| forces |
| consumer |
| vendor |
| base |

1 He started out as a .... selling hot dogs from a van.
2 We publish school textbooks, so our .... are the students.
3 We've built up a really strong .... over the past five years.
4 Their product is too expensive, so .... will soon make them drop the price.
5 She is the .... for the country's leading chain of shoe shops.

19.3
6 marks

Find the answer to each clue. Some letters have been given to help you.

1 The market .... is made up of buyers and sellers.
2 The market .... is how much buyers are willing to pay.
3 Producers are forced to sell what buyers want by market ....
4 The government doesn't fix prices in a market ....
5 An advertising company needs a strong .... base.
6 People who buy products for their own use are ....

1	p			c				
2		r		c				
3				s	s			s
4	e					y		
5	c	l						
6	c		n		m			

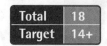
20.1
6 marks

Choose the best word to fill each gap. Put a circle around the letter, A, B or C, of the answer you choose.

1 We are well known in America, but now we want to .... the European market.
A compete   B entrance   C penetrate
2 The world's soft drinks market is .... by Pepsi and Coca-Cola.
A dominated   B segmented   C shared
3 We were .... out of business by the large supermarket chains.
A left   B driven   C abandoned
4 We bought out our only competitor so we could .... the market in coffee.
A corner   B front   C edge
5 Our most important market .... is men aged from 18 to 30.
A place   B share   C segment
6 Competition is .... in the fast food business.
A efficient   B intense   C successful

20.2
6 marks

Complete each sentence by writing in the gap the correct form of the verb given in brackets ( ).

1 In the late 1990s, market .... in the field of computers was incredible.   (grow)
2 Our company is the market .... in financial software in the UK.   (lead)
3 Today our market .... is about 60% and it is still growing.   (share)
4 We investigated market .... and found that there are two main types of user for our product – small to medium companies and private individuals.   (segment)
5 We can't relax because we face stiff ....   (compete)
6 Our next target is to become a key .... in the US market.   (play)

20.3
6 marks

Find the answer to each clue to complete the crossword. Some letters have been given to help you.

Across
1 Enter a market
3 Abandon a market
6 To be the only seller

Down
2 Competitor
4 Intense
5 Not tough: _ _ _-key

	1		n		2			
		3			v			4
5								
6	o		p			z		
								c

Your score
/18

21.1
6 marks

Choose the best word or phrase to fill each gap. Put a circle around the letter, A, B or C, of the answer you choose.

Our company makes wooden garden furniture – mainly tables and chairs. Sales are much higher this year because we have spent a lot on (1) .... First we did a survey to find out about customer (2) .... Then we redesigned all our (3) .... to include the special (4) .... that people want. Our (5) .... included a competition in all the major gardening magazines where the prize was a set of our furniture. Most importantly, we've made sure all our (6) .... are very competitive because our customers want value for money.

1 A selling   B distributing   C marketing
2 A wants   B needs   C uses
3 A products   B benefits   C services
4 A goods   B profits   C features
5 A presenting   B promotion   C persuasion
6 A prices   B costs   C charges

21.2
6 marks

Complete each sentence by writing the correct word in each gap. Some letters have been given to help you.

1 We advertise on TV, but that's not enough. We need a whole new marketing c o n _ _ _ _ _ .
2 We need to tell customers about the special b e n _ _ _ _ _ _ that our service provides.
3 Our company is market-o r i _ _ _ _ _ _ . Everything we do is about giving buyers what they want.
4 The p a c _ _ _ _ _ _ _ doesn't only protect the goods – it advertises them too.
5 I've been a m _ _ k _ _ _ r for ten years and I know how to promote any product.
6 People in different parts of the country buy different things, so 'p _ _ _ e' is one of the four Ps of marketing.

21.3
6 marks

Choose the best word from the brackets ( ) to fill the gap.

1 You can't maximize sales unless you get the marketing .... right.   (mix/change)
2 Our company is market-........................... and so we regularly talk to focus groups.
                                         (promoted/driven)
3 The new model has lots of new .... including air-conditioning.   (services/features)
4 Jim Scott is in charge of .... our new range mobile phones.   (promoting/orienting)
5 Our travel service offers customers many .... including free insurance.
                                         (characteristics/benefits)
6 If your business is not market-........................... , you may find that your product doesn't sell.
                                         (fed/led)

Your score
/18

Products and brands

22.1
6 marks

Match each statement to a word pair from the list. Write the letter of your chosen answer next to the statement. There is one word pair that you don't have to use.

A product catalogue   B consumer durables   C generic products
D product placement   E brand image   F brand recognition   G product lifecycle

1 If you want a big Hollywood star to wear a shirt with your company's logo on in a film, it will cost you over one million dollars.	
2 The latest edition contains pictures, descriptions and prices of everything that we sell.	
3 In a survey, 72% of shoppers identified our product before those of our competitors.	
4 The dishwashers, washing machines and dryers we produce have three-year guarantees.	
5 We aim to sell 500,000 units in the first year. Then sales will drop quickly to about 15,000 a year. We'll have to launch a new model in four years' time.	
6 Customers buy supermarket own-label versions rather than branded products because they offer better value for money.	

22.2
6 marks

Choose the best word from the brackets ( ) to fill the gap.

1 Our product .... includes tables, chairs and cupboards.   (group/portfolio/package)
2 I've always bought Ford cars and I love their new ....   (mark/make/model)
3 We will be launching a new product .... early next year.   (brand/cycle/line)
4 We want our brand .... to be young, fast and exciting.   (picture/image/logo)
5 Fast-moving .... goods, such as fresh food, have to be sold quickly.
                                        (consumer/customer/client)
6 The purple colour we use on all our labels is a key part of our ....
                                        (branding/marking/positioning)

22.3
6 marks

In each numbered line, there is *one* word which is *wrong*. Circle the mistake and write the correct word at the end of the line. The first one is an example.

0 Our (branding) name is recognized throughout Europe.   *brand*
1 We make men's clothes and our product mixture includes shirts, trousers   ....
2 and jackets. Next year's product ranger will also include hats and shoes.   ....
3 We have a clear brand identify. Our customers see our clothes as modern, ...
4 but also well made. Our product depositing is between the famous fashion   ....
5 labels of Italy and the owner-brand products of UK high street shops.   ....
6 To maintain brand aware, we advertise in men's lifestyle magazines.   ....

Your score
/18

Total 22
Target 15+

23.1
10 marks

Draw a line from each word on the left to a word on the right to make a word pair. (There is one extra word that you don't have to use.) Then use your word pairs to complete the sentences below.

price	price
list	cut
up	level
bottom	end
entry	loss
	market

1 Our basic range of tennis rackets is priced at the .... of the market.
2 For example, our .... racket for beginners is just £20.
3 Last year, the .... for our most expensive model was £250.
4 But after last week's .... it is now just £200.
5 Lots of people start with one of our cheaper rackets and then move ....

23.2
7 marks

Choose the best word to fill each gap from the alternatives given below. Put a circle around the letter, A, B or C, of the word you choose.

Homestead is a new company selling consumer durables at low prices. The company has a policy of permanently low (1) .... In fact, they guarantee that all branded products will be at least 10% less than the recommended (2) .... price. For example, a washing machine listed at £380 is on sale at £320. That's a (3) .... of over 15%. Competitors are angry that the company is using loss (4) .... to attract customers. A spokesperson for Homestead admitted that some products were being sold at a (5) .... but argued that this is standard business practice. 'They just don't like the fact that we are (6) .... them,' he added. Is this the start of a price (7) .... ?

1 A charging	B pricing	C trading
2 A retail	B sale	C cost
3 A charge	B profit	C discount
4 A dealers	B leaders	C traders
5 A loser	B lost	C loss
6 A undercutting	B discounting	C overpricing
7 A hike	B war	C tag

23.3
5 marks

Find the answer to each clue. One or two letters are given in each case.

1 When prices are rising quickly: a price ....
2 Not cheap and not expensive
3 Small, specialized market
4 Goods between basic and sophisticated
5 Buy a better model than the one you have

1	b							
2	m		–	p				
3	n							
4	m		–	r				
5	t				u			

24.1
8 marks

Find the word from the list below that *best* fits each statement. Write the letter of your chosen answer next to the statement. There is one extra word that you don't have to use.

1 We buy large quantities of wine directly from the producers and sell to shops and restaurants.	
2 We have a small shop selling newspapers, magazines, sweets and cigarettes.	
3 We opened in Chicago in 1952. We sell coffee, sodas and pastries. And, of course, medicines!	
4 I own the Pizza Express restaurant in our town. I get a lot of help from the parent company.	
5 It is a huge shop and it sells everything – food, clothes, furniture, plants, everything.	
6 We sent out 200,000 letters to car owners last week promoting our new insurance service.	
7 We phone people between 6 and 8 in the evening trying to sell them home security products.	
8 Most big towns in England have a shopping centre but the idea came from the US.	

A telemarketing   B mall   C discounter   D hypermarket   E drugstore
F mailshot   G wholesaler   H retailer   I franchise

24.2
10 marks

Draw a line from each word on the left to a word on the right to make a word pair. (There is one extra word that you don't have to use.) Then use your word pairs to complete the sentences below.

chain	marketing
deep	centre
direct	calls
cold	store
call	precinct
	discounters

1 Mailshots, telemarketing and door-to-door selling are all part of ....
2 We have about 150 telesales people in our .... in Dublin.
3 We use .... to find new customers but most people don't like being approached by companies that they don't know.
4 The bigger supermarkets don't like .... because they offer very low prices.
5 The 'Body Shop' is a .... with branches throughout the UK.

24.3
6 marks

Find the answer to each clue. The first letter is given in each case.

1 Disapproving term for direct mail: .... mail
2 A shop can also be called a retail ....
3 Disapproving term for wholesalers
4 Type of store that sells a wide range of goods
5 Local shop that's open long hours: .... store
6 Wholesalers and retailers are ....

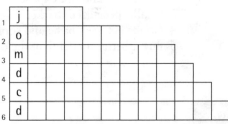

Promotion

25.1
6 marks

Complete each sentence by writing in the gap the correct form of the verb given in brackets ( ).

1 I work for a large .... agency.   (advertise)
2 We have placed a full-page display .... in every national newspaper.   (advertise)
3 Product .... is very effective if you use a really big sports star.   (endorse)
4 This year we will spend about 2 million dollars on ....   (sponsor)
5 The .... of our new product range starts next week.   (promote)
6 The first prize in our .... is a week's holiday in Spain.   (compete)

25.2
10 marks

Draw a line from each word on the left to a word on the right to make a word pair. (There is one extra word that you don't have to use.) Then use your word pairs to complete the sentences below.

sales	samples
special	offer
free	product
loyalty	territory
cross	promotion
	card

1 We sent .... of our new shampoo to 100,000 homes for people to try.
2 When a customer shows her .... she gets a 2% discount.
3 We use .... so, for example, if you buy our toothpaste you get a special deal on our toothbrushes.
4 My .... covers the north of England and Scotland.
5 The .... on this product range ends on the first of September.

25.3
6 marks

Choose the best word from the brackets ( ) to fill the gap.

1 I think that a TV commercial is the best advertising ....   (place/medium/agency)
2 Our magazine offers readers a free .... every month.   (prize/discount/gift)
3 We value the men and women of our ....   (salesmen/salespeople/sales force)
4 I'm running the advertising .... for the launch of our new model.
                          (campaign/endorsement/promotion)
5 I'm Sally Forbes and I'm .... manager for Iceberg Frozen Foods.
                                (sells/sales/selling)
6 Most of the .... who use our newspaper are small, local businesses.
                          (advertisers/adverts/advertising)

Your score
/22

The Internet and e-commerce

26.1
10 marks

Choose the best word to fill each gap from the alternatives given in the box below. There are some words that you don't have to use.

I'm Justin and I run a chain of bookshops specializing in old and rare books. Last year we started an e- (1) .... operation. It's been very successful. We have about 4,000 unique (2) .... and last month our home page had over 15,000 (3) .... Visitors use the site's search (4) .... to look for book titles or authors. They add items to their shopping (5) .... and, when they've finished, they pay (6) .... using a credit card. We send the books out by post so we don't have any (7) .... mile problems like some companies. Since we started (8) .... we've had more customers in our traditional (9) ....-and-mortar shops. People see our site while they are (10) .... the web and that persuades them to come along.

hits	cart	page	engine	securely	e-tailing	surfing	
users	clicks	bricks	first	last	commerce	procurement	

26.2
6 marks

In each sentence, there is *one* word which is *wrong*. Circle the mistake and write the correct word at the end of the line.

1 E-port is the country's latest Internet serving provider.   ....
2 It gives free Internet excess to registered users.   ....
3 You can open an accountant by visiting E-port's website.   ....
4 The first thing to do is to get your user word from the ISP.   ....
5 Then you enter a secret passport so that only you can log on.   ....
6 Now you can explore the World Wild Web at any time.   ....

26.3
9 marks

a) **Complete the meaning of each abbreviation.**
b) **Decide whether each statement is about B2C, B2B or B2G. Tick (✓) the right box.**

B2C: business to ....   B2B: business to ....
B2G: business to ....

	B2C	B2B	B2G
1 Members of the public can buy train tickets online.			
2 Last year we paid our business tax directly over the Internet.			
3 We order all our office stationery from our supplier on the web.			
4 All our workshops use e-procurement for the spare parts they need.			
5 We applied for the contract after seeing the details on the Ministry's website.			
6 I order my contact lenses over the Internet and pay with my credit card.			

Your score
/25

Sales and costs

27.1
8 marks

Choose the best word from the brackets ( ) to fill the gap.

1 The new model will be .... sale in July.   (at/on/in)
2 The shop was having a .... so I got these shoes at half price.   (sale/sales/sell)
3 It's easy to .... a sale if the product's good and the price is right.   (do/make/give)
4 Last month, ... sales reached nearly 1500.   (unit/piece/number)
5 Sales last month were below our .... of €120,000.   (gross/target/share)
6 Staff salaries are included in our .... costs.   (direct/indirect/overhead)
7 Our basic model has a selling .... of £28.   (cost/margin/price)
8 We estimate that sales .... next year will be about 5%.   (growth/forecast/volume)

27.2
6 marks

**Choose the best word to fill each gap from the alternatives given in the box below.
There are some words that you don't have to use.**

'I've just finished .... the new computer we are launching next year. Direct
.... costs will be $480. I estimate our .... to be about $20. That gives
.... costs of $500. We want a ....-up of about 20% so the sale price
will be $600. That gives a .... margin of nearly 17%. Not bad.'

forecast	production	costing	total	profit	mark	revenue	overheads

27.3
8 marks

Find the answer to each clue. The first and last letters are given in each case.

1 Selling price minus total costs: .... margin
2 Abbreviation for the variable costs in making goods
3 Selling price minus direct costs: .... margin
4 Number of things sold: sales ....
5 Money received from sales
6 Money received from sales (another word)
7 Another word for indirect costs
8 Estimate of next year's sales

1	n		t		
2	c			s	
3	g				s
4	v				e
5	r				e
6	t				r
7	e				s
8	f				t

Profitability and unprofitability

28.1
5 marks

Look at the costs and prices of these lamps. Choose the best word from the brackets ( ) to fill the gap in each sentence that follows.

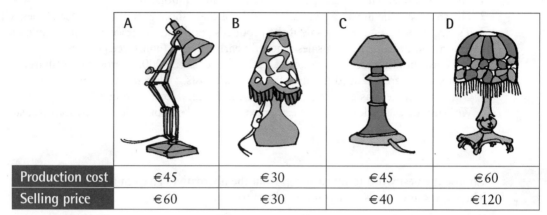

	A	B	C	D
Production cost	€45	€30	€45	€60
Selling price	€60	€30	€40	€120

1 We make a .... of €15 on lamp A.   (budget/expense/profit)
2 We .... even on sales of lamp B.   (break/make/take)
3 We make a .... on lamp C.   (lose/loss/lost)
4 Lamp D is very popular. It's a real ....-spinner.   (cash/finance/money)
5 We are going to stop making lamp C because it's just not ....
                                                    (profitable/saleable/valuable)

28.2
5 marks

Choose the best word to fill each gap from the alternatives given in the box below.
There are some words that you don't have to use.

'My name is Ann Morgan and I'm Advertising Manager at Gissing PLC. Last year, I had an advertising .... of £1,000,000. Our .... on TV adverts was £800,000 and £400,000 went on placing display ads in magazines. So our actual .... was £1,200,000. That means that we .... by £200,000. The Director of Finance was not pleased and I have been told that I must not be .... budget again next year.'

expenditure	expenses	budget	under	over	spend	overspent	underspent

28.3
6 marks

Write one word in each gap to complete the sentences.

1 We sell 15,000 of this model a year and make $80 on each one. It's a real _ _ _ _cow.
2 I overspent because I didn't budget _ _ _ the repair of the photocopier.
3 We reach break-even _ _ _ _ _ when we've got ten buyers. After that, everything is profit.
4 We sell this product at less than cost price. Loss _ _ _ _ _ _ _ like this attract customers into the shop.
5 The big supermarkets benefit from _ _ _ _ _ _ _ _ _ of scale because they get low prices from suppliers.
6 Since we set up the business two years ago we've been on a steep _ _ _ _ _ _ _ _ curve.

Getting paid

29.1
9 marks

Choose the best word from the brackets ( ) to fill the gap in each sentence.

1 You have to .... the furniture directly from the manufacturer.   (ask/order/require)
2 Your order is now ready and we will .... it tonight.   (plane/train/ship)
3 We send the invoice to the customer's .... address.   (billing/receipting/costing)
4 We have a strict credit .... : all accounts to be paid in 28 days.
(police/policy/politics)
5 I have a serious cash .... problem because they haven't paid me.
(credit/expense/flow)
6 You must send your tax form to the .... Revenue tomorrow.
(Inland/Inside/Inboard)
7 They are never going to pay the £200 they owe me so I've .... it off.
(signed/written/posted)
8 Our payment .... are cash or cheque when the goods are delivered.
(terms/words/notes)
9 In the US, 'accounts .... ' refers to customers that owe the company money.
(deductible/payable/receivable)

29.2
5 marks

In each of the numbered sentences (1–5) there is *one* word which is *wrong*. Circle the mistake and write the correct word at the end of the line.

Our company supplies stationery and office equipment.
1 Customers put their orders by phone or over the Internet.   ....
2 Nearly all orders are displaced within 24 hours.   ....
3 We give business customers trade debit with 30 days to pay.   ....
4 Most people pay on time but some still own us money after six months.   ....
5 Last year we had bad depths worth over £10,000.   ....

29.3
6 marks

For each sentence, find *one* word to replace the underlined phrase. Write the word at the end of the sentence.

1 I look after our large and important accounts.   _ _ _
2 I'm also responsible for chasing people who owe us money.   _ _ _ _ _ _ _
3 We always pay our suppliers and other people we owe money to on time.   _ _ _ _ _ _ _ _ _
4 We give our best customers a 10% reduction in the price they have to pay.   _ _ _ _ _ _ _ _
5 We don't give credit so our customers have to pay before they receive the goods.

_ _ _ _ _ _ _
6 We raise an invoice and send it to the customer immediately.   _ _ _ _ _ _ _

Your score
/20

Assets, liabilities and the balance sheet

30.1
6 marks

Choose the best word from the brackets ( ) to fill the gap in each sentence.

> ## RETAIL BUSINESS FOR SALE:
> ## £125,000
>
> 1 Newsagent's shop for sale as a going ....   (business/concern/outlet)
> 2 .... assets include shop, fittings and a new   (Permanent/Firm/Fixed)
>   delivery van.
> 3 The estimated .... value of these assets is   (book/invoice/paper)
>   £120,000.
> 4 .... assets include stock worth £15,000.   (Current/Present/Actual)
> 5 The most important .... asset is our good   (invisible/invaluable/intangible)
>   reputation.
> 6 The .... of our customers is included in   (goodness/goodwill/goodbye)
>   the asking price.

30.2
5 marks

Complete each of the numbered sentences (1–5) by writing one word in the gap. The first letter has been given to help you.

Over time, the equipment that a company owns loses value.
1 For example, computers and other IT equipment <u>d</u> _ _ _ _ _ _ _ _ very quickly.
2 When we do our accounts, we <u>a</u> _ _ _ _ _ _ _ them over three years.
3 So the value of a $6,000 PC is <u>w</u> _ _ _ _ _ down by a third in the first year.
4 The depreciation of $2,000 is shown as a <u>c</u> _ _ _ _ _ in our financial records.
5 Depreciation of all assets is shown on the <u>b</u> _ _ _ _ _ _ sheet at the end of the year.

30.3
5 marks

Choose the best word from the brackets ( ) to fill the gap.

1 Our .... include a €12,000 tax bill and the €8,000 we owe our suppliers.
   (assets/debtors/liabilities)
2 Our .... are valuable because they have good customer recognition.
   (brands/types/makes)
3 Company cars depreciate quickly. We write them .... completely after five years.
   (up/out/off)
4 Our .... year runs from the 1st of June to the 31st of May.
   (financial/revenue/capital)
5 Our only .... liability is a €10,000 bank loan to be paid off over five years.
   (current/long-term/fixed)

Your score
/16

The bottom line

31.1
8 marks

Choose the best word to fill each gap from the alternatives given below. Put a circle around the letter, A, B or C, of the word you choose.

It was announced today that the chemical giant Emronia UK is to be investigated. This follows an (1) .... which revealed problems in the company's (2) .... A company spokesperson said that annual (3) .... for the past five years had given a (4) .... and fair picture of Emronia's financial position. He stressed that the company follows British accounting (5) .... But expert commentators are not convinced. Last year, Emronia reported a pre-tax (6) .... of £29.6 million but many think that this was due to (7) .... accounting – or worse. Giles Merchant, advisor to the Stock Exchange, said that the company was haemorrhaging red (8) .... but had hidden the size of its liabilities.

1 A amortization   B accountancy   C audit
2 A accounts   B assets   C credits
3 A books   B records   C reports
4 A false   B good   C true
5 A results   B rules   C firms
6 A profit   B budget   C line
7 A window   B creative   C direct
8 A blood   B ink   C losses

31.2
5 marks

Match each word in Box A with one word from Box B to make five word pairs. (There is one word in Box B that you don't have to use.) Then use your word pairs to complete the sentences below.

Box A	window	accounting	bottom	exceptional	book
Box B	line	standards	account	keeper	loss	dressing

1 The .... shown in our year's accounts was due to the purchase of a new shop.
2 The .... used in the US are different from those in Europe.
3 At the moment, I'm a .... but I'm training to be an accountant.
4 There was no escaping the .... ; a net loss of €35,000.
5 After a little bit of .... , our figures for this year look a lot better.

31.3
5 marks

In each sentence, there is *one* word which is *wrong*. Circle the mistake and write the correct word at the end of the line.

1 My name is Jane Morton and I am an accountancy in London.   ....
2 I prepare the end-of-year accounting for several small businesses. ....
3 They send me their records and I draw up a profit and lost account. ....
4 This shows the growth profit and any charges against the company.   ....
5 When these are taken away, you are left with your netting profit for the year. ....

Your score
/18

32.1
12 marks

Choose the best word to fill each gap from the alternatives given below. Put a circle around the letter, A, B or C, of the word you choose.

When I started my engineering company five years ago I had to (1) .... a lot of capital. First, I looked around for a (2) .... and took out a loan. The (3) .... was £100,000 at an (4) .... rate of 5.2%. I had to use my house for (5) .... so that was a big worry. Next I found ten people who wanted to (6) .... in the business. Each one put (7) .... £10,000 in return for 1,000 shares. I (8) .... 12,000 shares so I am the biggest shareholder. Our total (9) .... is nearly a quarter of a million pounds. We paid our first (10) .... last year but it wasn't very big. Now we are making a profit, we will start to reduce our (11) .... I don't like carrying this much (12) ....

1 A rise	B raise	C rose		7 A out	B up	C off
2 A lender	B borrower	C capitalist		8 A hold	B pick	C hand
3 A money	B balance	C principal		9 A gearing	B venture	C equity
4 A account	B interest	C audit		10 A division	B divider	C dividend
5 A security	B safety	C salary		11 A borrowing	B lending	C sharing
6 A lend	B borrow	C invest		12 A capital	B debt	C collateral

32.2
5 marks

Decide which of the alternatives (A–H) each speaker is talking about. Write the letter of your answer in the box at the end of the sentence. There are some alternatives that you don't have to use.

1 'We had to find a lender who was prepared to finance an exciting new company.'	
2 'Our lending to companies takes the form of conditional loans or debentures.'	
3 'If you do not keep up with the repayments, we may sell your home to recover our money.'	
4 'The company is highly geared so I wouldn't invest in it.'	
5 'We owe our suppliers $12,000 and we have a loan of $8,000 so the total is about $20,000.'	

A indebtedness   B equity   C share capital   D bonds
E leverage   F gross profit   G venture capitalist   H collateral

32.3
5 marks

Complete each sentence by writing in the gap a noun formed from the verb given in brackets ( ). The first one is an example.

0 We charge each ......*borrower*...... a fee of £200 to arrange a loan. (borrow)
1 This year we will pay a .... of 25¢ per share. (divide)
2 To get the loan we had to use the new lorry as .... (secure)
3 We are looking for a .... who offers reasonable interest rates. (lend)
4 Their debts have grown steadily and now their .... is dangerously high. (gear)
5 I think that our .... is now under control. (borrow)

Your score
/22

Read the questions carefully. Try to answer them all. This test takes about 45 minutes.

1
12 marks

For each sentence, choose the best word to fill the gap from the alternatives given. Put a circle around the letter, A, B or C, of the word you choose.

1 We do our printing in-house but we .... delivery to a small, local company.
  A supply   B source   C subcontract

2 We have set up quality .... as part of our TQM system.
  A circles   B lines   C corners

3 We need a .... market economy where the government doesn't try to control prices.
  A base   B low   C free

4 Until last year they .... the market but now they face some stiff competition.
  A penetrated   B dominated   C segmented

5 Our new .... protects our eggs on the way to the shops and it looks good on the shelves.
  A production   B packaging   C promotion

6 If you want to save some money buy .... products rather than the top brands.
  A generic   B durable   C consumer

7 If you pay cash for this TV we will give you a 5% ....
  A hike   B sale   C discount

8 Our prices are low because we cut out the .... and sell directly from the factory.
  A middleman   B marketer   C manufacturer

9 Customers who use our .... card get one point for every pound they spend.
  A franchise   B sponsorship   C loyalty

10 We had nearly 5,000 .... to our website last week.
  A hits   B visitors   C views

11 We can increase our profit .... by reducing our overheads.
  A account   B margin   C costs

12 We've made a loss for the past three years but we should break .... this year.
  A even   B up   C out

2
6 marks

Match each sentence beginning (1–6) with the correct ending. Write the letter (a–g) of the ending you choose in the box below. There is one extra ending that you don't have to use.

1	Our only long-term liability is	a	profit of $1.2 million for last year.
2	Syntectic PLC reported a pre-tax	b	the learning curve has been very steep.
3	We fell behind with our repayments so	c	we can sell the stock in our warehouse.
4	Next time I'm going to trade up to	d	they started undercutting us.
5	Now we've got the product right, but	e	a £5,000 bank loan over three years.
6	We'll solve our cash flow problem if	f	they sold the house we'd put up as collateral.
		g	something at the high end of the range.

Answers	1	2	3	4	5	6 ....

Choose one word from the box to complete each sentence. There is one word that you don't have to use.

in	out	on	off	against	up	under	over

1 I need an investor to put .... the money for the new machinery.
2 IT equipment depreciates quickly so we amortize it .... three years.
3 They weren't going to pay so I had to write it .... as a bad debt.
4 The accounts show that the company is .... the red.
5 I didn't spend as much as expected and I was .... budget by €12,000.
6 BMW's new model will be .... sale in January next year.
7 The competition was so fierce we were driven .... of the market.

Draw a line from each word on the left to a word on the right to make a word pair. (There is one extra word that you don't have to use.) Then use your word pairs to complete the sentences below. The first one is an example.

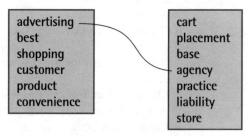

advertising — cart
best   placement
shopping   base
customer — agency
product   practice
convenience liability
            store

0 We use a professional ......*advertising agency*........ to run our marketing campaigns.
1 It may work, but .... in a Hollywood movie costs a fortune.
2 We wanted to improve our efficiency so we looked at .... in the US.
3 Our local .... is open 24 hours a day, seven days a week.
4 Our large and loyal .... is our most valuable, intangible asset.
5 Just select what you want from our e-store and put it in your virtual ....

Complete the sentences below by writing one word in each gap. The first letter is given to help you.

1 We get the raw m _ _ _ _ _ _ _ _ for our furniture from south-east Asia.
2 Our products are not for the mass m _ _ _ _ _ but for a small, exclusive niche.
3 We want consumers to associate our b _ _ _ _ name with value for money.
4 I think that TV is the most powerful advertising m _ _ _ _ _ .
5 If salaries rise then our direct c _ _ _ _ will eat up all our profits.
6 You should include the value of the building and all the equipment in your fixed a _ _ _ _ _ _ .
7 We check on customer service by sending mystery s _ _ _ _ _ _ _ into our stores.
8 The Inland Revenue wants to see our profit and loss a _ _ _ _ _ _ for last year.

6

6 marks

In each sentence, there is *one* word which is *wrong*. Circle the mistake and write the correct word at the end of the line. The first one is an example.

0   We are the market (ladder) with a 48% share of consumer spending.   ......*leader*......

1   Always try to satisfy customer wants and you'll be successful.   ....

2   We supply parts to car manufacturers on a just-off-time basis.   ....

3   To keep quality high we do spotting checks throughout the day.   ....

4   Retailers buy from holesalers and then sell on to their customers.   ....

5   Our site has a search machine so you can look for key words.   ....

6   Last year, our sales turnout was 5% higher than our forecast.   ....

7

6 marks

Match each headline to a statement. Write the number of the statement you choose in the box next to the headline. (There is one statement that you do not have to use.)

Global Net is market leader ☐   **Board faces dividend fury** ☐   **No end to housing price boom** ☐

Time to invest in a franchise? ☐   **Music e-tailer records profit** ☐   **Anglia Boats to move upmarket** ☐

1   The new 'Elite' range will have higher specifications and be aimed at buyers with more than £200,000 to spend.

2   The company announced that it is to issue more shares in order to raise capital for its expansion.

3   Last year, their share of the market rose to 34% – almost 3% higher than their biggest competitor.

4   The advantage is that you own the shop, but the parent company provides stock, advertising and advice.

5   Shareholders were shocked to hear that they would receive just 2¢ for every share as a result of the company's poor performance last year.

6   The survey shows that average prices rose by 2% last month making the annual rise a massive 18%.

7   The company reported that their online sales service had moved out of the red for the first time.

8

8 marks

Write the abbreviations below in words. Some words and letters have been given to help you.

1   ISP   Internet S_____   P_____

2   B2G   Business To G_____

3   COGS   Cost Of G____   S____

4   FMCG   Fast M_____   C_____ Goods

5   BPR   Business P_____ Re-engineering

Match each statement to one of the financial terms given below. Write the letter (A–H) in the box next to the statement. There are some terms that you don't have to use.

1 We owe our suppliers $15,000 for building materials.	
2 Our salary bill last year was $280,000.	
3 It was $20,000 new, but now its book value is about $10,000.	
4 We spent $30,000 on rent, electricity and insurance for this office.	
5 So, after paying interest, tax and everything else, we made $150,000.	
6 We've just agreed a bank loan for $50,000 payable over ten years.	

A direct costs   B creditors   C net profit   D depreciation
E overheads   F debtors   G gross profit   H long-term liability

For each sentence, find *one* word to replace the underlined phrase. Write the word at the end of the sentence.

1 Juan will be in charge of <u>designing, promoting and getting stores to stock</u> our new
   product range.   ....

2 Our new <u>book containing descriptions and prices of all our products</u> will be
   sent out next week.   ....

3 We do not give customers <u>a period of time before they have to pay</u>.   ....

4 We act as <u>outside accountants who check financial records</u> for several
   major companies.   ....

5 Choose a top-end model and we will give you a
   10% <u>reduction in the price you have to pay</u>.   ....

6 You log on to the site using a <u>secret word that only you know</u>.   ....

> **This is the end of Summary Test 2.**
> **Use the Answer key at the back of the book to check your answers.**

33.1
5 marks

Choose the best word to fill each gap from the alternatives given in the box below.
There are some words that you don't have to use.

Bad news for shareholders of Barloni PLC. Jacky Lai, the CEO appointed last year, has failed to turn .... the ailing company and last month it defaulted .... its huge $1.2 million debt. There is no hope of finding anyone to bail .... Barloni so it will be put .... receivership next week. When the company is wound .... , shareholders will get almost nothing.

up	before	out	into	at	round	from	on

33.2
6 marks

Choose the best word to fill each gap from the alternatives given below. Put a circle around the letter, A, B or C, of the word you choose.

Alicom is a successful company. For the past ten years it has (1) .... part of its profits as dividends. However, its (2) .... earnings have been considerable. Its cash (3) .... are now estimated to be around €20 million. Financial experts say that Alicom has only a small debt to (4) .... and so may use its cash (5) .... to buy out one of its rivals. CEO, Angela White, said that the company has no immediate plans to make an (6) .... , but that it couldn't be ruled out in the future.

1 A posted	B distributed	C retailed
2 A retained	B stored	C kept
3 A shares	B burden	C reserves
4 A file	B default	C service
5 A stock	B mountain	C hill
6 A acquisition	B administration	C application

33.3
7 marks

In each line there is *one* word which is *wrong*. Circle the mistake and write the correct word at the end of the line.

1 We need time to reorganize our finances so we're filing for bankruptness. ....
2 That should protect us from our credits for at least six months. ....
3 The truth is we have a debt cries which has been building up for years. ....
4 Yesterday we asked the bank to schedule our debt over ten years. ....
5 If they don't agree, then the company will collide immediately. ....
6 We will have to cease traiding and make all our staff redundant. ....
7 If the bank says yes, then I think that we can make a full recover. ....

Your score
/18

Mergers, takeovers and sell-offs

34.1
9 marks

Choose the best word from the brackets ( ) to fill the gap in each sentence.

1 I have a 20% .... in a small printing company.   (invest/interest/input)
2 Charles Wilson now has a majority .... in Alicom PLC.   (hold/holder/holding)
3 ProSports and Fit Folk gave details of their new joint ....
                                                   (venture/account/combine)
4 Kola-Co has made a .... bid of 21p per share.   (kind/friendly/gentle)
5 Buying out the contracts of senior executives will be a poison .... for any predator
   to swallow.   (medicine/tablet/pill)
6 Eastern Water proved to be our white .... saving us from collapse.
                                                   (angel/knight/saint)
7 Their .... company is a multinational based in New York.   (parent/father/family)
8 We started as a music company but we .... into television.
                                         (diversified/diverted/differed)
9 We do many things but our .... activity is publishing.   (concern/centre/core)

34.2
5 marks

In each of the numbered sentences (1–5) there is *one* word which is *wrong*. Circle the mistake and write the correct word at the end of the line.

Our manufacturing company is small but it has lots of assets.
1 We are worried that we may be pray to a big multinational.   ....
2 Last year, Anders Holdings made a hostage bid for us.   ....
3 They wanted to ackquier us as their subsidiary in Europe.   ....
4 We didn't want to be part of a huge conglomerus so we rejected the bid.   ....
5 We are now considering a murger with another small engineering firm.   ....

34.3
6 marks

For each sentence, find *one* word to replace the underlined phrase. Write the word at the end of the sentence. The first two letters have been given to help you.

1 The problem is that the company is <u>not concentrating on a few important things</u>.
                                                   u n _ _ _ _ _ _ _
2 Robert Bateson now has a <u>bigger than 50%</u> stake in English Petroleum. m a _ _ _ _ _ _
3 I think that <u>selling off non-core assets</u> is necessary to save the company. d i _ _ _ _ _ _ _ _
4 Europe Airways has formed an <u>arrangement to work together</u> with Alpha Airlines.
                                                   a l _ _ _ _ _ _
5 Global Electric's latest <u>company that it has bought</u> is Cambridge Electra. a c _ _ _ _ _ _ _ _ _
6 At the moment, we just make shoes but we want to <u>start doing business in other areas</u>.
                                                   d i _ _ _ _ _ _ _

Personal finance

35.1
6 marks

Decide which of the alternatives (A–H) each speaker is talking about. Write the letter of your answer in the box at the end of the sentence. There are two alternatives that you don't have to use.

1 'You get your own cheque book so, for example, you can pay your bills by post.'	
2 'We borrowed £80,000 from the building society to buy our house.'	
3 'I do all my shopping using plastic and then I pay when I get my monthly statement.'	
4 'It's in both our names so we can both get money out when we want.'	
5 'We are nearly £200 in the red and we are paying a lot of interest on it.'	
6 'We've got about £2,000 saved and the bank pays about 4% interest on it.'	

A credit card   B current account   C overdraft   D joint account
E debit card   F deposit account   G mortgage   H bank statement

35.2
10 marks

Choose the best word to fill each gap from the alternatives given below. Put a circle around the letter, A, B or C, of the word you choose.

'My name is Jenny Logan and I'm in charge of e-banking at ScotWest Bank. We have local (1) .... like all the other (2) .... banks, but more and more of our customers are using the Internet. Our "Internet only" savings account allows customers to (3) .... their money 24 hours a day. You can check your account (4) .... day or night and, if you want, (5) .... money from one account to another. You don't get a (6) .... book but you can pay bills electronically. Also we don't send a bank (7) .... through the post every month because you can print one off at any time. Internet banking is very efficient so our (8) .... are lower and we pay more (9) .... on e-accounts. At the moment the (10) .... is 4%.'

1 A shops	B branches	C outlets		6 A cheque	B credit	C cash
2 A high-street	B top-end	C mid-range		7 A report	B statement	C invoice
3 A arrange	B manage	C audit		8 A charges	B debits	C credits
4 A profit	B total	C balance		9 A overdraft	B dividend	C interest
5 A dispose	B distribute	C transfer		10 A level	B rate	C share

35.3
5 marks

Write one word in each gap to complete the sentences.

1 We have about $10,000 invested in u _ _ _ trusts.
2 If our building society is demutualized, everyone will get a w _ _ _ _ _ _ _ of £250.
3 The government says that it can't afford to increase the s _ _ _ _ pension by more than 1%.
4 I am lucky because I am a member of the company pension s _ _ _ _ _ _ .
5 Thousands of small i _ _ _ _ _ _ _ _ lost money when the share price collapsed.

Your score
/21

36.1
6 marks

Decide which of the alternatives (A–H) each speaker is talking about. Write the letter of your answer in the box at the end of the sentence. There are two alternatives that you don't have to use.

1 'This is New York's financial centre.'	
2 'We bought euros at $0.94 and sold at $0.98.'	
3 'If I want, I can buy 10,000 shares at $2 in 12 months' time.'	
4 'The government has borrowed £50 billion over a ten-year period.'	
5 'Our contract is to buy 500 ounces of gold at $420 in 30 days, so we hope the price rises.'	
6 'The traders here deal in metals, wheat, rice, orange juice – things like that.'	

A Square Mile   B forex   C bourse   D futures contract
E Wall Street   F commodities exchange   G bonds   H options contract

36.2
6 marks

Complete each sentence by writing in the gap a word formed from the verb given in brackets ( ).

1 This bank is one of London's oldest .... institutions.   (finance)
2 We deal mainly in commodities and .... (derive)
3 We have about 60 .... buying and selling stocks.   (deal)
4 The .... of the company raised £1.4 million.   (float)
5 A .... wants to make a quick profit.   (speculate)
6 I invest in .... – mainly stocks and bonds.   (secure)

36.3
6 marks

Choose the best word to fill each gap from the alternatives given below. Put a circle around the letter, A, B or C, of the word you choose.

Pegasus Software looks like a good buy. The company was (1) .... last year and its shares are (2) .... on the London stock (3) .... When they were (4) .... , they were valued at 60 pence. Lots of (5) .... were attracted by the company's strong sales figures. Now the (6) .... is worth 92 pence.

1	A bonded	B floated	C raised
2	A quoted	B signed	C noted
3	A bourse	B city	C exchange
4	A issued	B started	C distributed
5	A auditors	B creditors	C investors
6	A trade	B stock	C deal

Your score
/18

Trading

37.1
8 marks

Choose the best word to fill each gap from the alternatives given below. Put a circle around the letter, A, B or C, of the word you choose.

'The bad news for investors continues. Today the Dow, the NASDAQ and the European
(1) .... all showed heavy loses. Prices on the London FTSE fell to a five-year (2) ....
with banks and insurance companies showing spectacular (3) .... Dealers are pessimistic
and no one can see an end to this (4) .... market. Over the past month we have seen more
than $20 billion (5) .... off the value of US stocks. The only good news from Wall Street
was a small rise in blue (6) .... just before the (7) .... This late (8) .... helped the
Dow to finish just half of one per cent lower on the day.'

1 A	indices	B prices	C lists		5 A	waved	B washed	C wiped
2 A	crash	B low	C barrier		6 A	chips	B stocks	C shares
3 A	declines	B trades	C demands		7 A	finish	B shut	C close
4 A	bull	B bear	C buffalo		8 A	record	B rally	C recover

37.2
6 marks

In each line there is *one* word which is *wrong*. Circle the mistake and write the correct word at the end of the line.

1 In Tokyo today, turnoff was very high – especially in the hi-tech sector.   ....
2 More than half a billion shares changed arms in six hours.   ....
3 There was a lot of demanding for shares in microchip manufacturers.   ....
4 Siltel, in particular, made spectacular ganes and was up 8.5% on the day.   ....
5 The Nikkei 225 broke through the 10,000 bar for the first time this year.   ....
6 Experts are confident that this bull index will continue for some time.   ....

37.3
5 marks

Write one word in each gap to complete the sentences.

1 He lost all his money in the stock market _ _ _ _ _ of 1987.
2 Microsun's share _ _ _ _ _ rose to $4 yesterday – its highest for two years.
3 The New York _ _ _ _ _ of 'new economy' shares is the NASDAQ.
4 There was _ _ _ _ _ selling in Frankfurt with dealers trying to sell shares at any price.
5 Yesterday, more than 3% of total market _ _ _ _ _ _ _ _ _ _ _ _ _ _ was lost on Wall Street.

38.1
6 marks

Choose the best word from the brackets ( ) to fill the gap.

1 The country's .... is very strong at the moment. (finance/economy/balance)
2 All the economic .... are positive. (indicators/index/inputs)
3 The gross .... product is at an all time high. (domestic/deficit/discount)
4 We also have a trade .... of over £16 billion. (benefit/share/surplus)
5 The annual inflation .... is below 2%. (growth/rate/gap)
6 The number of people out of .... is less than 400,000. (job/employ/work)

38.2
5 marks

Complete each sentence by writing in the gap a word formed from the verb given in brackets ( ).

1 She is an expert in .... management. (finance)
2 The country's gross national .... grew by 10% last year. (produce)
3 The level of .... is high because companies have cut jobs. (employ)
4 Higher wages will increase .... pressure in the economy. (inflate)
5 Our .... rate was nearly 10% last year. (grow)

38.3
6 marks

Find a word related to each clue. The first letters of the answers are given.

1 Dealing with very large sums of money: .... finance
2 Value of a country's products and services:
   economic ....
3 Goods sold abroad
4 Unemployed
5 Rising prices
6 Cheap to buy and to use

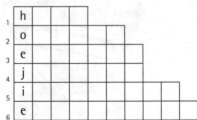

1 h					
2 o					
3 e					
4 j					
5 i					
6 e					

Your score
/17

39.1
8 marks

Choose the graph (A–E) which best fits each sentence. You can use each graph more than once.

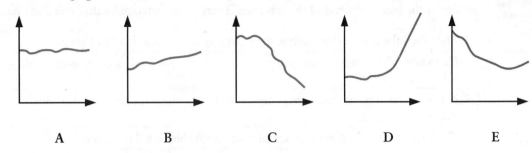

A   B   C   D   E

1 'Oil prices skyrocketed last week as fears over supplies grew.' ....
2 'The dollar–euro exchange rate remains steady at about 0.98.' ....
3 'Telecom shares plummeted on warnings of bad sales figures.' ....
4 'The FTSE 100 fell yesterday but bottomed out at 7,900.' ....
5 'Adventi Corporation shares advanced to $2.80.' ....
6 'Sales at Super Mart have stagnated over the past year.' ....
7 'Micro Sun shares soared yesterday on news of a possible bid.' ....
8 'The Hang Seng dived yesterday and closed at a five-year low.' ....

39.2
8 marks

Choose the best word from the brackets ( ) to fill the gap.

1 The CAC 40 .... at 3,051 before falling back to 2,992. (advanced/peaked/soared)
2 Anglia Agro .... to 121 pence from a high of 123. (eased/leapt/jumped)
3 Our share price rose in the morning but then it levelled .... at 62 pence. (up/down/off)
4 Internet dealers say they will .... the price of a new car by over 10%. (slash/slump/bust)
5 It's not bad enough to call it a slump, but we are in a .... (depression/repression/recession)
6 .... means that growth is slow, but prices are rising quickly. (Stagnation/Stagflation/Inflation)
7 United Foods announced it is going to .... 1,500 jobs. (axe/dive/close)
8 As temperatures rise, the .... for air-conditioning units increases. (boom/surge/demand)

39.3
4 marks

Find a word related to each clue. The first letters of the answers are given.

1 A period of very strong growth
2 When production falls, growth is ....
3 A very bad slump
4 Opposite of a peak

1	b						
2	n						
3	d						
4	t						

Your score
/20

40.1
6 marks

Decide which of the alternatives (A–G) each speaker is talking about. Write the letter of your answer in the box at the end of the sentence. There is one alternative that you don't have to use.

1 They used the profits from selling drugs to buy houses and land in Europe.	
2 He moved £200 from the company account to his own bank account every week for years.	
3 Net Rail and West Trains secretly agreed to charge the same fares on their busiest routes.	
4 The $100 note was so good it was almost impossible to tell it from a real one.	
5 They offered him $20,000 to give the contract to them and not their rivals.	
6 The CEO was arrested because she sold all her shares just before the price plummeted.	

A price fixing   B insider trading   C money laundering   D counterfeiting
E bribery   F racketeering   G embezzlement

40.2
6 marks

Complete each sentence by writing in the gap a word formed from the verb given in brackets ( ).

1 They thought the President was involved in ....   (corrupt)
2 Publishing lies about a company to push down its share price is market ....   (rig)
3 He was found guilty of insider .... last year.   (deal)
4 He was accused of .... because he gave politicians cash for favours.   (bribe)
5 They made a lot of money .... famous brand sports wear.   (fake)
6 She organized the .... of postage stamps worth $2 million.   (forge)

40.3
5 marks

In each of the numbered sentences (1–5) there is *one* word which is *wrong*. Circle the mistake and write the correct word at the end of the line.

My name is Laura Rayner and I work for the Finance Sector Authority.
1 Our job is to regular banking and investment services.   ....
2 We look at reports of wrongdone in companies.   ....
3 Some cases are small – like a director taking a 'sweetness' for a favour.   ....
4 Others are very serious. One scram involved a man who sold $1 million   ....
5 worth of shares in a company that didn't exist! That's frawd.   ....

Your score
/17

41.1
9 marks

Choose the best word to fill each gap from the alternatives given below. Put a circle around the letter, A, B or C, of the word you choose.

'My name is Peter Gill. I manage the One World (1) .... investment fund. We follow a very clear (2) .... of conduct when we choose stocks. We only invest in companies that are socially (3) .... so we don't put money into tobacco companies or arms manufacturers. Green (4) .... are very important to us. We check that our companies are not damaging the (5) .... We invest in some companies that make their products in countries where (6) .... is cheaper, and we make sure that they do not (7) .... their workers. Some expensive, famous brand clothing is made in (8) .... where people work long hours for very low wages. We think that is completely (9) ....'

1	A honesty	B ethical	C rights
2	A note	B list	C code
3	A responsible	B spectacular	C interested
4	A issues	B actions	C indexes
5	A neighbours	B environment	C local
6	A work	B job	C labour
7	A export	B employ	C exploit
8	A sweatshops	B sweatshirts	C sweetshops
9	A moral	B unethical	C social

41.2
6 marks

Complete each sentence by writing one word in each gap. Use the words in brackets ( ) to help you.

1 We expect everyone in this company to behave e _ _ _ _ _ _ _ _. (ethics)
2 We regularly discuss e _ _ _ _ _ _ issues with managers and workers. (ethics)
3 Last year we put in place an a _ _ _ _ _ _ _ _ _ _ action programme. (affirm)
4 This helps us to avoid sexual and racial d _ _ _ _ _ _ _ _ _ _ _ _ _. (discriminate)
5 Many of our employees are green a _ _ _ _ _ _ _ _. (active)
6 They take direct action on a wide range of e _ _ _ _ _ _ _ _ _ _ _ _ issues. (environment)

42.1
8 marks

There is *one* word which is *wrong* in each of the numbered sentences (1–8). Circle the mistake and write the correct word at the end of the line.

I'm Eddy Yeung and I'm in charge of building this bridge.
1 The leader time for preparing this project was six months. ....
2 We drew up a three-year frametime for the work to be completed. ....
3 At the end of one year, everything was on scheduling. ....
4 Then there was a delayment because an important machine broke down. ....
5 We had nearly two months of uptime while it was repaired. ....
6 As a result, we are now a long way before schedule. ....
7 We are working hard to make out time but it is not easy. ....
8 You know how it is. Everything takes long than planned. ....

42.2
6 marks

Look at the chart for building a house. Use the information in the chart to complete the sentences below. Write one word in each gap. The first letter is given to help you.

		March	April	May	June
1	Clear site				
2	Build walls				
3	Put on roof				
4	Services: water				
5	Services: electricity				
6	Decorating				
7	Hand over				

1 The t............... for this project is four months.
2 The first s............... is clearing the site.
3 Putting in the water and the electricity run in p............... .
4 Phases 4 and 5 o............... with the period for decorating.
5 C............... is scheduled for the last week of June.
6 The builder will get a b............... payment if the project is finished early.

42.3
5 marks

Find the word that completes each tip on time management. The first and last letters of the answers are given.

1 Use a diary or a .... to plan your week.
2 If you like computers, use an electronic personal ....
3 Put the things you need to do in order – .... them!
4 Don't be .... , and avoid interruptions.
5 Balance .... with time. Don't aim for perfection.

1	c					r
2	o					r
3	p					e
4	d					d
5	q				y	

Your score
/19

Stress and stress management

Total	18
Target	14+

43.1
6 marks

For each sentence, find *one* word to replace the underlined phrase. Write the word at the end of the sentence. The first two letters have been given to help you.

1 I'm a nurse because I want to do something <u>that gives me a lot of satisfaction</u>.

r e _ _ _ _ _ _ _

2 I work hard but my job is very <u>interesting and makes me feel good</u>.   s t _ _ _ _ _ _ _ _ _

3 My new job is <u>difficult but in an interesting way</u>.   c h _ _ _ _ _ _ _ _

4 Now I'm a manager I feel <u>that things are difficult and there's a lot to do</u> at work.

s t _ _ _ _ _ _ _

5 I started to feel <u>that I couldn't deal with all the pressures of work</u>.   o v _ _ _ _ _ _ _ _ _

6 My last boss left the job because of <u>very bad tiredness and stress</u>.   b u _ _ _ _ _

43.2
6 marks

Choose the best word from the brackets ( ) to fill the gap in each sentence.

1 I don't like working .... stress.   (behind/under/over)
2 My doctor said my illness was stress-............................. .   (induced/involved/input)
3 I don't think I can deal with the stresses and .... at work.   (surges/stretches/strains)
4 He had a .... breakdown last year but he's much better now.

(nerve/nervy/nervous)

5 I have to get out of the rat .... before I am burned out.   (race/trap/cage)
6 This job is so competitive I feel as if I'm on a ....

(timeframe/treadmill/sweatshop)

43.3
6 marks

In each of the numbered sentences (1–6) there is *one* word which is *wrong*. Circle the mistake and write the correct word at the end of the line.

I've decided to give up my job in the city and move to the country.
1 I've been completely stressed outwards and it is damaging my health.   ....
2 I'm so overemployed that I am too tired to sleep at night.   ....
3 That's why I'm going to change my lifestyling.   ....
4 I want to spend some qualification time with my family.   ....
5 Lots of people in London are thinking about backshifting.   ....
6 They're all looking for a life that is unstrainful.   ....

Leadership and management styles

44.1
10 marks

Choose the best word to fill each gap from the alternatives given below. Put a circle around the letter, A, B, C or D, of the word you choose.

'My name is Laura Garcia and I train people in modern management techniques. Old style managers were (1) .... They took all the decisions and told their (2) .... what to do without talking to them. They were often very (3) .... from their employees. They (4) .... their decisions from above and their whole approach was (5) .... and (6) .... A modern manager has to be more (7) .... and (8) .... Decision-making needs to be (9) .... so everyone should be involved in the process of (10) ....'

1 A authority	B authorized	C authoritarian	D authorizing
2 A subordinates	B superiors	C sponsors	D speculators
3 A above	B further	C long	D remote
4 A imported	B imposed	C stressed	D pressured
5 A bottom-up	B upside-down	C inside-out	D top-down
6 A bureaucratic	B administrative	C organized	D restructured
7 A closed	B shut	C over	D open
8 A advanced	B relaxing	C approachable	D distant
9 A decentralized	B unfocused	C depreciated	D restructured
10 A talking	B consultation	C speaking	D discussing

44.2
5 marks

Complete each sentence by writing in the gap a word formed from the verb given in brackets ( ).

1 I like people in this company to use their ....   (initiate)
2 We believe in .... so we let people control their own work.   (delegate)
3 .... means letting people make their own decisions.   (empower)
4 We discuss things and even argue but then we reach a ....   (consent)
5 I'm going on a course to develop my .... skills.   (lead)

44.3
4 marks

Find the words that match the clues. The first and last letters of the answers are given.

1 Talent
2 Energy and drive
3 Attractive quality that good leaders have
4 Leader who can see what the future will be like

1	f			r			
2	d					m	
3	c					a	
4	v						y

45.1
8 marks

Decide which of the alternatives (A–F) each speaker is talking about. Write the letter of your answer in the box at the end of the sentence. You will have to use some alternatives more than once.

1 'All CEOs over the age of 50 use an authoritarian approach to management.'	
2 'The top people were all men and they encouraged an aggressive management style.'	
3 'Our organization has five levels of management.'	
4 'Here we consult employees on all major decisions. We work by consensus.'	
5 'The people on the shop floor say that our managers don't have any leadership skills.'	
6 'I want the people who work for me to be tough. If they are weak they can leave.'	
7 'I like all the people in my team to call me Steve rather than Mr Eastwood.'	
8 'Women make better managers than men because they are better with people.'	

A corporate culture   B macho culture   C canteen culture
D hierarchical structure   E form of address   F stereotype

45.2
5 marks

Write one word in each gap to complete the sentences.

1 We involve everyone in the decision-_ _ _ _ _ _ process.
2 This is not a hierarchical company. We only have two management _ _ _ _ _ _ .
3 We work as a team of _ _ _ _ _ _ . The newest employee's ideas are just as important as mine.
4 The _ _ _ _ - hours culture here puts people under pressure.
5 I like it here because the company _ _ _ _ _ _ _ is to encourage people to use their initiative.

45.3
5 marks

In each line there is *one* word which is *wrong*. Circle the mistake and write the correct word at the end of the line.

1 Our new manager is very open and approachive.   ....
2 We can be family with him, but we still respect him.   ....
3 My last manager was distant and remove.   ....
4 He was not excessable and he didn't ask for our opinions.   ....
5 We had to show him difference even if we did not agree with him. ....

Business across cultures 2

46.1
6 marks

Choose the best word to fill each gap from the alternatives given below. Put a circle around the letter, A, B or C, of the word you choose.

'My name is Daniel Bertolino and I'm a software developer. In our department, we dress
(1) .... We can't wear shorts or dirty T-shirts so I suppose it's "(2) .... casual". People
in Sales have to dress (3) .... The men wear dark business (4) .... and so do the
women. They all look the same. It's like a (5) .... really. At the end of each month we have a
(6) .... Friday. It's strange to see the CEO without a tie on.'

1 A casualty   B causally   C casually
2 A smart   B straight   C special
3 A obligatory   B remotely   C formally
4 A shirts   B suits   C suites
5 A uniform   B portfolio   C logo
6 A dress-up   B dress-down   C dress-in

46.2
10 marks

Look at the business cards and labels. Decide whether each statement is 'True' or 'False'. If there is not enough information to decide, tick (✓) the 'Does not say' box. Then answer questions 8–10.

Mrs Paula Howard M.A.
Customer Services

Provector Insurance
PO Box 274
Ipswich, IP41 6HJ
Tel: 01473 262626

King Media PLC
1 High Street, Cambridge, CB1 2EU

Charles Caspar
Chief Executive Officer
Tel: +44 1223 662200
E-mail: caspar.c@kingmedia.co.uk

William J Davenport Sr.
Vice President, Finance
Global Foods Inc.

Sarah A Moreland BSc, MBA
Head of Marketing

	True	False	Does not say
1 Paula Howard is married.			
2 Charles Caspar doesn't have any qualifications.			
3 William Davenport has a son called William.			
4 Mr Davenport's middle name could be Robert.			
5 Paula Howard doesn't have a middle name.			
6 If you meet the CEO of King Media, you should call him Mr Charles.			
7 If you write to Sarah, you could address her as 'Ms S. Moreland'.			
8 What is the family name of the person who works for Provector?	....		
9 What qualifications does Sarah Moreland have?	....		
10 What is the surname of the CEO of King Media?	....		

Your score
/16

Business across cultures 3

47.1
5 marks

Draw a line from each word on the left to a word on the right to make a word pair. (There is one extra word that you don't have to use.) Then use your word pairs to complete the sentences below.

working	break
corporate	holiday
lunch	lunch
public	breakfast
eye	hospitality
	contact

1 Make .... with customers so that they know you are listening.
2 I usually go shopping during my ....
3 Tomorrow is a .... so the office will be closed.
4 Let's discuss this over a .... tomorrow morning.
5 We spent over $40,000 last year on ....

47.2
6 marks

Choose the best word to fill each gap from the alternatives given in the box below. There is one extra word that you don't have to use.

1 Our overseas clients expect .... when they visit so I take them out every evening.
2 He is very keen on .... , so get there early.
3 I don't like .... lunches because they go on for too long.
4 There was a culture of .... with people at their desks even at the weekend.
5 You can learn a lot from watching the .... that people make when they are talking.
6 An important business meeting is not the place for .... It can go horribly wrong.

| presenteeism | punctuality | humour | business |
| absenteeism | gestures | entertainment | |

47.3
7 marks

In each line there is *one* word which is *wrong*. Circle the mistake and write the correct word at the end of the line.

1 When you meet someone, it is important to get the greet right. ....
2 I shake hands with people, but I don't really like physical contract. ....
3 In some cultures you should give pressants to everyone you meet. ....
4 You should also know the rules of conversion when you go to meetings. ....
5 It may be rude to enterrup people when they are talking. ....
6 Also, think about the role of silent. Is it rude to be quiet for long periods? ....
7 Finally, say 'Good buying' to everyone when you leave. ....

Your score
/18

Telephoning 1: phones and numbers

Total	27
Target	22+

48.1
10 marks

Decide which of the alternatives (A–H) each speaker is talking about. Write the letter of your answer in the box at the end of the sentence. You will have to use some alternatives more than once.

1 'Our meeting was in Paris but we linked up with Bill's team in the New York office.'	
2 'It's an oh-eight-hundred number so you don't have to pay.'	
3 'Good morning, Washington. Good afternoon, Oslo. Can you all see and hear us?'	
4 'Yes, she's in her office. I'll put you through to her now.'	
5 'If I'm not in the office, call me on my mobile.'	
6 'You have to put in at least 20 pence before you can make a call.'	
7 'The picture is not very good but it's nice to see who you're talking to over the Internet.'	
8 'To order at this special price, call our sales team on 01776 223344 – now!'	
9 'I take it with me in the car. But I don't use it when I'm driving.'	
10 'If you have any problems, call our technical team on 01473 123123.'	

A cellphone   B webcam   C videoconference   D helpline
E hotline   F Freephone   G extension   H payphone

48.2
9 marks

Choose the best word from the brackets ( ) to fill the gap.

1 I'm out tomorrow morning, so give me a .... in the afternoon.
                             (call/phone/telephone)
2 I like this .... phone because I can use it in the garden.
                            (moveable/cordless/extended)
3 If they need me at work, they send a message on my .... (pager/reader/text)
4 I have one .... for my phone and another for my Internet connection.
                                  (wire/cord/line)
5 Jim phoned from Los Angeles. Can you call him .... tomorrow? (out/up/down)
6 We have a call .... in Dublin that deals with customer enquiries.
                            (office/centre/site)
7 Customers in the States can call us on our ....-free number. (toll/cost/price)
8 Give me a .... if you want to go to the conference next week. (ping/bing/ring)
9 There's a public phone where you can use coins or a phone .... (card/note/ticket)

48.3
8 marks

Write the telephone numbers below in figures. The first one is an example.

'one – seven – six, three – two – three – three'	176 3233
'oh – one – double two – three, five – six – oh – four – double nine'	
'oh – eight hundred, double seven – double one – double seven'	
'double four, one – eight – one, three – zero – three – zero'	
'one – eight hundred, double five – double five – double five'	

Your score
/27

Telephoning 2: getting through

49.1
17 marks

Here are some things you might hear on the phone. Write one word in each gap to complete the messages and conversations.

1 'Call me at the office tomorrow. My .... line is 01202 818335. If I'm not there, leave a message on my .... and I'll call you .... when I get in.'

2 'All international lines are .... Please .... up and try again later.'

3 'Can I speak to Anita Singh, please?'

'Oh, I'm sorry. She's not on this .... ; she's on 227. I'll put you through to the main .... Just ask the .... to transfer you to the Sales Department.'

4 'Good morning. You are .... to the King's Theatre ticket hotline. How can I help you?'

'Oh, I think I've got the .... number. I wanted 470401.'

'Ah, yes. This is 470410.'

5 'Hello, operator. Can you check a number for me? It's 077 23 23 23. I was talking to someone there but I got .... off. Now when I call, I just get the .... tone.'

6 'Hello, Reception? Can you tell me how to make a call to France?'

'Certainly, sir. Just pick up the phone and .... "9" to get a line. When you hear the .... tone, dial 00 33 and then the number you want in France.'

7 'This is the Freedom Credit Card helpline. To check your balance, please press "1" on your .... To make a payment, press "2".'

8 'Hi, Alex. This is Mario. I got your message yesterday, but I was busy so I couldn't .... your call. Sorry I missed you. I'll call .... later.'

50.1
9 marks

Here are three telephone conversations. Choose the best word from the brackets ( ) to complete each sentence.

■ Good morning. This is Pierre Cognet. Could I .... to Mr Roberts, please?
(tell/speak/phone)

○ I'm .... he's in a meeting.   (afraid/scared/unfortunate)

■ Ah. Could I .... a message?   (ask/send/leave)

○ Of course.

■ Could you ask him to call me .... ? My number's 33-1-4776-5821.
(back/down/round)

○ OK. I'll tell him you called.

■ Thank you.

■ Hello. Is that Anna?

○ ....   (Saying/Talking/Speaking)

■ Hi, Anna. This is Alain. Is this a .... time to call?   (fine/good/best)

○ Not really, Alain. Could you call back .... ?   (late/lately/later)

■ OK. I'll call back after lunch.

○ That's great. Bye.

■ Hello. Is that Sven Anderson?

○ No. Sven's not in the office today. Can I .... a message?   (make/take/place)

■ Oh, I'm calling .... tomorrow's meeting. I wanted to confirm that it starts at 10.
(about/for/to)

○ Yes, it does. I'll be there too.

■ Ah, good. Thank you. I'll see you tomorrow then. Bye.

○ See you tomorrow. Bye.

50.2
5 marks

Here are some telephone conversations where one speaker is checking some information. Tick (✓) the correct option. The first one is an example.

'Did you say your extension is 607?' 'Six – oh – double seven.'	607	6077 ✓
'Is that with one N or two at the end?' 'It's double N.'	Hermann	Herman
'Is that all one word?' 'No. It has a hyphen.'	thompsonclarke@aol.com	thompson-clarke@aol.com
'Do you know if that's with a capital V?' 'He writes it with a small letter.'	Van Lent	van Lent
'Was that a P or a B?' 'It's Bravo Alpha 471.'	BA 471	PA 471
'Can you repeat the address, please?' 'It's www dot art dot house dot org, forward slash music.'	www.art.house.org/music	www.arthouse.org\\music

Your score
/14

Telephoning 4: arrangements

Total	22
Target	16+

51.1
11 marks

Here are two telephone conversations. Write one word in each gap to complete the sentences. The first letter has been given to help you.

■ Nick, I'm calling to see if we can f............................ a meeting for next week.
○ OK. I'll just c............................ my diary.
■ What a............................ Tuesday?
○ Sorry. I've got t............................ go to a meeting in London.
■ Could you m............................ Wednesday?
○ No problem. Let's s............................ Wednesday at 10 then.
■ OK. I look f............................ to seeing you then. Bye.
○ See you, Nick.

....

■ Hello, Ali. It's Maria. Would it be useful for us to meet next week?
○ Yes, I think so. Would Thursday be s............................ for you?
■ I won't be a............................ to make Thursday, I'm afraid.
○ OK then, let's meet on Friday at 9.
■ That's f............................ . I'll see you then.
○ OK, Maria. Thanks for c............................ .

51.2
11 marks

Here are two voicemail messages. Choose the best word from the brackets ( ) to complete each sentence.

1 | Jacques. It's Paul. I can't .... next Monday's meeting after all.
(being/make/arrive)
Something has come .... and I have to fly to Frankfurt.   (out/down/up)
.... Tuesday be possible for you?   (Would/What/Why)
If not, we'll have to _____ it off until the week after.   (let/take/put)
I'll be in _____ soon. Bye.   (touch/calling/speak)

2 | Ellen. It's Stefan. I'm afraid the 22nd won't be ....
(possibility/possible/possibly)
I'm sorry, but I've .... to go to Oslo.   (have/must/got)
We're going to have to put it .... for at least a week.   (back/out/behind)
I'm completely .... under with the Woodstock contract.
(rained/snowed/stormed)
Can we leave it .... for the time being?   (open/shut/fixed)
Talk to you .... no doubt. Bye.   (now/then/soon)

Your score
/22

Read the questions carefully. Try to answer them all. This test takes about 45 minutes.

1
12 marks

For each sentence, choose the best word to fill the gap from the alternatives given.
Put a circle around the letter, A, B or C, of the word you choose.

1 The company's debt .... was too large and it couldn't make the repayments.
   A schedule   B default   C burden
2 With 51% of the shares, Max Com now has a .... interest in Media World.
   A majority   B mid-range   C minority
3 We agreed a £4,000 .... with the bank but the interest rate is very high.
   A deposit   B overdraft   C balance
4 Geno Science was .... on the stock exchange last year.
   A issued   B floated   C invested
5 The FTSE 100 .... fell by 1.4% yesterday.
   A market   B bourse   C index
6 I've got lots to do but finishing this report is my first ....
   A priority   B schedule   C perfection
7 The Japanese car manufacturer is to .... 5,000 jobs at its plants in Europe.
   A axe   B plunge   C ease
8 He was selling Rolex watches for $1,000, but they turned out to be ....
   A counterfeits   B forges   C fakes
9 The country's gross domestic .... has grown by more than $200 billion.
   A payment   B product   C profit
10 I gave up my job in the City to have more .... time with my family.
   A downshift   B value   C quality
11 Our new CEO has charisma and a natural .... for leadership.
   A flair   B drive   C energy
12 I think that .... is important so I am never late for a business meeting.
   A hospitality   B formality   C punctuality

2
6 marks

Match each sentence beginning (1–6) with the correct ending. Write the letter (a–g) of the ending you choose in the box below. There is one extra ending that you don't have to use.

1	If we are late completing the project	a	because I prefer to meet people face to face.
2	I got through to Ivan in Moscow	b	that we are thinking of downshifting.
3	Work has become so stressful	c	so I've got to put off our meeting.
4	Something has come up	d	then we will have to pay a penalty.
5	I don't really like videoconferencing	e	if the bank won't reschedule our debt.
6	The market had another difficult day	f	but then I got cut off.
		g	and was nearly 2% down at the close.

| Answers | 1 .... | 2 .... | 3 .... | 4 .... | 5 .... | 6 .... |

3

7 marks

Choose one word from the box to complete each sentence. There is one word that you don't have to use.

behind	up	over	under	in	out	on	off

1 ScotNat Bank has agreed to bail .... the troubled company with a £1 million loan.
2 Renée Latour has a 15% stake .... the country's biggest wine exporter.
3 We have a $20,000 loan which we are paying .... over two years.
4 Ampost Inc. is quoted .... the New York stock exchange.
5 Megacorp shares advanced in heavy trading and finished 85¢ .... at $7.35.
6 There was a delay and now we are four weeks .... schedule.
7 I have been .... stress at work and now I'm off sick.

4

10 marks

Draw a line from each word on the left to a word on the right to make a word pair. (There is one word that you don't have to use.) Then use your word pairs to complete the sentences below. The first one is an example.

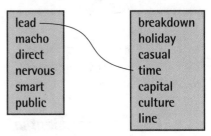

lead	breakdown
macho	holiday
direct	casual
nervous	time
smart	capital
public	culture
	line

0 This project had a .....*lead time*..... of about 12 months.
1 He had a .... and I think it was due to stress at work.
2 Monday is a .... in Thailand so the Bangkok office will be shut.
3 Call me on my .... – 01344 246246.
4 The sales team has a .... and everyone is expected to be forceful.
5 The dress code is .... so I don't have to wear a suit.

5

8 marks

Complete the sentences below by writing one word in each gap. The first letter is given to help you.

1 The country's inflation <u>r</u> _ _ _ was almost 15% last year.
2 United Bank's new deposit <u>a</u> _ _ _ _ _ _ pays interest of 4.2%.
3 Blue <u>c</u> _ _ _ _ saw strong gains on Wall Street yesterday.
4 I called the helpline at least ten times, but every time I got the engaged <u>t</u> _ _ _.
5 She was arrested yesterday on charges of insider <u>d</u> _ _ _ _ _ _.
6 The two airlines announced their joint <u>v</u> _ _ _ _ _ _ after the meeting.
7 A top-down <u>a</u> _ _ _ _ _ _ _ to decision-making makes employees feel that they are not valued.
8 I didn't trust him because he wouldn't make eye <u>c</u> _ _ _ _ _ _ with me.

6

In each sentence, there is *one* word which is *wrong*. Circle the mistake and write the correct word at the end of the line. The first one is an example.

0 Over the past three years, we've changed the company ⟨cult⟩ here. ......*culture*......

1 We are encouraging people to use their own initiate. ....

2 We want to power employees so we delegate responsibility. ....

3 We also want our people to be simulated at work – not stressed. ....

4 The company has a strict note of conduct which we all follow. ....

5 We hope that there is no racial or sexual decrimination here. ....

6 And a happy team is more productive. Last year sales sawed by 27%. ....

7

Match each headline to a statement. Write the number of the statement you choose in the box next to the headline. (There is one statement that you do not have to use.)

Top executives leave rat race ☐

Dress-down Friday ups productivity ☐

Mobiles increase stress says report ☐

Green investors grow in importance ☐

Sportswear giant in sweatshop claim ☐

CEO's backhander lands him in court ☐

1 Children work a 12-hour day for 50¢ making trainers that retail in the US at more than $150.

2 The research shows that employees who dress casually produce more than those in business suits.

3 Mr Trent took the cash in return for inside information about the company's merger plans.

4 The problem with perfection is that it can't be achieved – even if you work 24 hours a day.

5 The study shows that ethical investment increased at more than twice the market average last year.

6 More and more people are giving up jobs with huge salaries to move to a slower, more relaxed lifestyle.

7 They can't relax because the boss may call at any time of the day or night wherever they are.

8

8 marks

Choose the graph (A–E) which best fits each sentence. You can use each graph more than once.

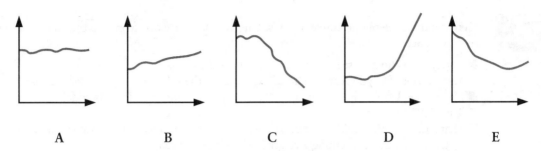

A   B   C   D   E

1 'The inflation rate has remained steady over the past year.' ....
2 'The NASDAQ plummeted yesterday as technology stocks were hit again.' ....
3 'The Infotel share price has skyrocketed on news of the merger.' ....
4 'London was a little more bullish yesterday and the FTSE 100 advanced to 8,050.' ....
5 'Exports to the US have stagnated over the past year.' ....
6 'Demand for cheap air travel has increased dramatically.' ....
7 'The CAC 40 has fallen recently but now seems to have bottomed out.' ....
8 'The trade surplus has been growing slowly but steadily over the past three years.' ....

9

6 marks

Match each statement with one of the financial terms given below. Write the letter (A–H) in the box next to the statement. There are some terms that you don't have to use.

1 We deal in investments in minerals, metals and agricultural produce only.	
2 There is a lot of optimism and dealers think share prices could soar.	
3 The all-share index plummeted by over 10% and is now at a 20-year low.	
4 We bought euros at $0.92 and sold them at 0.98.	
5 Things got better in the afternoon and, at the close, the Dow was up 0.5% on the day.	
6 I can, if I want, buy 10,000 company shares at £2 at the end of next year.	

A options contract   B bull market   C stock market rally   D capitalization
E foreign exchange   F bear market   G stock market crash   H commodities

10

6 marks

For each sentence, find *one* word to replace the underlined phrase. Write the word at the end of the sentence.

1 Experts think that this <u>period of negative growth</u> may last for another year. ....
2 She is a <u>person who buys and sells shares</u> in a securities house in New York. ....
3 I think that <u>the number of people who are out of work</u> is less than a million. ....
4 We found $2 million in <u>illegal copies of real</u> notes in his garage. ....
5 This project has a two-year <u>overall period for completing everything</u>. ....
6 We reach all decisions through a <u>process of asking employees what they think</u>. ....

> **This is the end of Summary Test 3.**
> **Use the Answer key at the back of the book to check your answers.**

Faxes

52.1
9 marks

Here are three telephone conversations. Choose the best word from the brackets ( ) to complete each sentence.

■ Pierre, I'm calling to see if you've finished the drawings.
○ Yes, Marina. Do you want me to .... them by fax?   (e-mail/send/post)
■ Yes, please. Do you have our fax .... ?   (number/address/code)
○ Is it 570 220?
■ That's it. Oh, and could you fax .... the specifications as well?   (my/me/mine)
○ I'll .... everything I've got.   (fax/faxing/faxed)
■ That'll be great. Thanks.
○ Bye, Marina.

15 minutes later

■ Pierre, it's Marina again.
○ Ah, Marina. Did you .... my fax?   (accept/get/have)
■ Yes, but the drawings weren't ....   (read/seen/legible)
○ OK, I'll .... them.   (resend/refax/receive)
■ Thanks, Pierre.

15 minutes later

○ Marina? Pierre here. Was everything OK?
■ The first ten pages were fine but then the machine ....   (fixed/stayed/jammed)
○ Ah, so you didn't get the specifications.
■ No. Can you send them .... again?   (through/out/around)
○ No problem. Let's hope it works this time.

52.2
8 marks

Complete each sentence using two words from the box below. There are two words that you don't have to use.

1 When you send a fax you must use the company's standard ....
2 You must be very careful when you send a fax containing ....
3 If you are not the .... of this fax, please phone 0207 271271.
4 If you do not receive all the pages, please .... the ....

advise	sheet	information	fax	sender
recipient	intended	machine	cover	confidential

Your score
/17

53.1
6 marks

An e-mail program has the options A–H as shown below. For each situation (1–6) choose the option that the user should choose. Write the letters of the options you choose in the boxes.

Address Book	Delete Message	Forward Message	Reply	Reply to All	Attach File	Start New E-mail	Send and Receive
A	B	C	D	E	F	G	H

1 Last week, Henri wrote an e-mail to his brother. Now he wants to get rid of it.	
2 Ivan got an important e-mail from a customer. He wants to send it on to his boss in Paris.	
3 Carla has received an e-mail from Vincent and she wants to send him an answer.	
4 Marie has a report saved on her computer. She wants to send it to John with the e-mail she has written.	
5 Stefan wants to check whether there are any e-mails waiting for him.	
6 Paula wrote an e-mail to Mike, Tim and Lee. Lee wants to send an answer to Paula and the others.	

53.2
8 marks

Look at the e-mail below. Then answer questions 1–3.

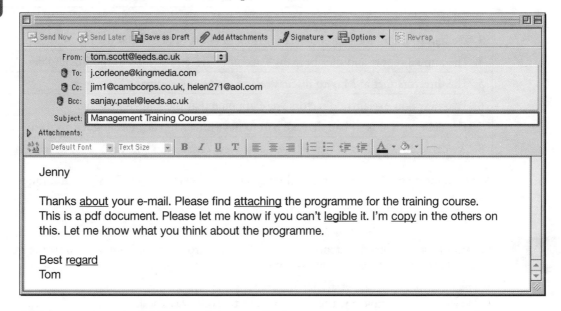

1 How many people did Tom send the e-mail to? ....

2 When Jenny gets this e-mail, will she see that Tom has sent a copy to Sanjay? How do you know? ....

3 In the message, the underlined words are wrong. Write the correct words in the table.

Wrong word	about	attaching	legible	copy	regard
Right word					

Your score
/14

Total 22
Target 18+

54.1
8 marks

Choose the best word from the brackets ( ) to fill the gap.

1 Can we .... up a meeting for early next week?   (arrange/set/agree)
2 I'm afraid I've got to bring .... this morning's meeting to ten o'clock.
(up/along/forward)
3 Something came up so they .... Monday's meeting till Friday.
(postponed/cancelled/fixed)
4 Anita is off sick so Michael will have to .... the staff meeting.   (charge/chief/chair)
5 I've got to .... the meeting in Paris because my boss will be in Spain.
(go/attend/visit)
6 It's a very important meeting so make sure you don't .... it.   (miss/lose/avoid)
7 On Friday we have a meeting .... our most important client.   (of/with/to)
8 It wasn't really a meeting – just an informal .... over coffee.   (speech/report/chat)

54.2
8 marks

Decide which of the alternatives (A–E) each speaker is talking about. Write the letter of your answer in the box at the end of the sentence. You will have to use some alternatives more than once.

1 'We tried to produce as many ideas as possible for the new marketing campaign.'	
2 'All the Sales team get together once a month to see how everything is going.'	
3 'We had to get all the shareholders together at short notice to discuss the merger plans.'	
4 'The annual report and the company's accounts were presented to the shareholders.'	
5 'The directors met in May to discuss restructuring the company.'	
6 'Two new non-executive directors were appointed at the annual meeting.'	
7 'The debt crisis was so bad that we had to have an emergency meeting for all members.'	
8 'We came up with lots of new ideas. Most were crazy but some are worth developing.'	

A board meeting   B departmental meeting   C AGM   D EGM   E brainstorming

54.3
6 marks

In each of the numbered sentences (1–6) there is *one* word which is *wrong*. Circle the mistake and write the correct word at the end of the line.

We had a project meeting yesterday to discuss progress.
1 They can be a complete waste of timing but this one was good.   ....
2 We had some useful discusses and cleared up some problems.   ....
3 Ahmed was chairing it and he kept things move along.   ....
4 When Sunita started to scramble, he brought her back to the point.   ....
5 Because there were no digressions we covered a lot of earth.   ....
6 I said I thought it was very producing and the others agreed.   ....

Your score
/22

Meetings 2: the role of the chairperson

Total	19
Target	16+

55.1
6 marks

Choose the best word to fill each gap from the alternatives given below. Put a circle around the letter, A, B or C, of the word you choose.

My name is Stuart Macintosh and I am personal assistant to the CEO of Eastern Oil. He is the (1) .... of the company's finance committee. I'm responsible for arranging the monthly meetings. I have to prepare the (2) .... and then I have to (3) .... it to all the participants. I also have to send copies of the (4) .... of the last meeting. It's my job to check the (5) .... , to make sure that the meeting room is suitable and that lunch has been ordered. You have to be a good (6) .... to do a job like this.

1 A chairlady   B chairperson   C chairwoman
2 A diary   B calendar   C agenda
3 A circulate   B circular   C circle
4 A hours   B minutes   C seconds
5 A avenue   B revenue   C venue
6 A organizer   B organized   C organization

55.2
8 marks

The statements below were made at a meeting. Write one word in the gap to complete each statement.

1 'Juliet, will you t.......................... the minutes today?'
2 'Does everyone agree that the minutes are an accurate r.......................... of the last meeting?'
3 'Are there any m.......................... arising?'
4 'In the a.......................... points it says Bob is responsible for writing the report. Is that right?'
5 'Now, we have a.......................... 30 minutes to the discussion of point 1, so let's get started.'
6 'I want to make the p.......................... that we are still two people short in the office.'
7 'We haven't r.......................... this issue so we'll discuss it next week and make a decision then.'
8 'Let's m.......................... on to the next point or we won't finish on time.'

55.3
5 marks

Find a word related to each clue. The first and last letters of the answers are given.

1 List of the things to be discussed at a meeting
2 Keep to this or the meeting will finish late
3 How the Chair should deal with disagreements
4 Someone who gets to the meeting after it has started
5 When someone goes off the point in a discussion

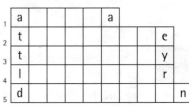

Meetings 3: points of view

56.1
7 marks

Choose the best word to fill each gap from the alternatives given below. Put a circle around the letter, A, B or C, of the word you choose.

'It's ten o'clock so let's make a (1) .... , shall we? As you are (2) .... , the main (3) .... of this meeting is to discuss the new marketing campaign. As I (4) .... it, the whole thing is too fancy and too expensive. I want to know what the (5) .... feeling is on this. What (6) .... you, Sam? Why don't you start the ball (7) .... ?'

1 A start   B begin   C first
2 A seeing   B knowing   C aware
3 A matter   B purpose   C action
4 A see   B look   C clear
5 A special   B general   C main
6 A for   B of   C about
7 A going   B rolling   C kicking

56.2
6 marks

In each line there is *one* word which is *wrong*. Circle the mistake and write the correct word at the end of the line.

1 I'd like to open the discuss about the new office design.   ....
2 As you knowing, each department is going to have an open plan office.   ....
3 In my opinions, that's a big mistake and we should think again.   ....
4 People work better, I belief, when they have their own space.   ....
5 Of coarse, some people may like it, but everyone in Finance is against it.   ....
6 What are your reviews on this, Amanda? Do you like the idea?   ....

56.3
6 marks

The statements below were made at a meeting. Write one word in the gap to complete each statement.

1 'OK. It's nine o'clock so let's get down to b........................ , shall we?'
2 'What is the o........................ of this meeting? What do we hope to achieve?'
3 'I've a........................ this meeting to discuss our debt crisis.'
4 'What are your f........................ on this, Ali?'
5 'It's perfectly c........................ to me that the decision has been taken already.'
6 'O........................ nobody wants to take a cut in salary, but we may have to.'

Your score
/19

Meetings 4: agreement and disagreement

Total	17
Target	14+

57.1
10 marks

Choose the best word to fill each gap from the alternatives given below. Put a circle around the letter, A, B or C, of the word you choose.

It's difficult chairing a meeting. When you have a (1) .... , some people will agree with you but others may (2) .... It's OK when it's just a (3) .... of opinion, but sometimes it turns into an (4) .... The important thing is to be (5) .... whatever happens. If someone gets very (6) .... or says something rude, keep (7) .... Just make your (8) .... but do not (9) .... your temper. If you are (10) .... , then things will just get worse!

1	A	discussion	B	percussion	C	repercussion
2	A	reply	B	refuse	C	disagree
3	A	different	B	difference	C	differently
4	A	agreement	B	argument	C	alternative
5	A	courteous	B	mistaken	C	absurd
6	A	disagreed	B	anger	C	angry
7	A	calm	B	cold	C	clear
8	A	place	B	part	C	point
9	A	lend	B	lose	C	let
10	A	perfect	B	absolute	C	impolite

57.2
7 marks

Complete each statement using one of the words from the box below. (There is one extra word that you don't have to use.) Then decide whether the statement expresses strong agreement (SA), mild agreement (MA), mild disagreement (MD) or strong disagreement (SD). Put a tick (✓) in the right box. The first one is an example.

	SA	MA	MD	SD
0 I'm ......*afraid*...... I can't agree with you there, John.			✓	
1 You're .... right. We have to reduce our prices.				
2 I'm sorry, Helen, but that's out of the				
3 Precisely. I couldn't .... more.				
4 I .... so, but I'd like to see the latest figures.				
5 That's .... I can't believe you want to pay just £4 an hour.				
6 I can't really go .... with that. I think your figures may be wrong.				
7 You may be .... there. Let's see what happens.				

along   disagree   question   suppose   afraid   absurd   agree   right   · perfectly

Your score
/17

Meetings 5: discussion techniques

58.1
7 marks

The statements below were made at a meeting. Write one word in the gap to complete each statement.

1 'I take your p......................... about the new logo, but it's too late to change it now.'
2 'I know what you m........................ about Marco, but he is very good with the customers.'
3 'I can see where you're c......................... from on this, but I still want to see the numbers.'
4 'Sorry to i......................... you, but what you've said is against company policy.'
5 'To go back to what I was saying e......................... , we still need to borrow £10,000.'
6 'If I u......................... you correctly, we will not finish the project on time. Is that right?'
7 'Are you s......................... that we should close the Oxford office?'

58.2
10 marks

Choose the best word to fill each gap from the alternatives given below. Put a circle around the letter, A, B or C, of the word you choose.

'Ladies and gentlemen, it's nearly five o'clock. We're (1) .... out of time so we're going to have to (2) .... there. Just to (3) .... up, we came here to decide whether to close the Oxford office or not. I've listened to both (4) .... of the argument and it is clear that we have not (5) .... an agreement. There is no (6) .... at this point so we will just have to agree to (7) .... for the moment. The working group will try to find a (8) .... and we will present its suggestions at the next meeting. That's on September 24th at nine o'clock. So, (9) .... anyone has anything else to add, I'll bring the meeting to a close. Thank you all for (10) ....'

1 A walking	B running	C moving		6 A senses	B census	C consensus
2 A stop	B stay	C still		7 A disagree	B argue	C discuss
3 A add	B equal	C sum		8 A compromise	B promise	C compound
4 A faces	B edges	C sides		9 A because	B unless	C until
5 A made	B reached	C worked		10 A attend	B being	C coming

58.3
6 marks

For statements 1–6 below, decide whether the speaker is hedging (H), interrupting (I) or concluding (C). Put a tick (✓) in the right box.

	H	I	C
1 'Well, I think that's it. Let's leave it there.'			
2 'Can I come in here, Lauren?'			
3 'I understand what you're saying, but I still think it would be difficult.'			
4 'OK. Let's go over what's been said.'			
5 'I see what you mean, but what about the costs?'			
6 'If I can just stop you for a moment, Justin.'			

Your score
/23

Presentations 1: preparation and introduction

59.1
7 marks

Decide which of the alternatives (A–F) each speaker is talking about. Write the letter of your answer in the box at the end of the sentence. You may have to use an alternative more than once.

1 'Professor Gillian Beer will give a paper entitled "Business Models for the 21st Century".'	
2 'We'll invite journalists from all the national papers and the top financial magazines.'	
3 'After Terry's speech, we'll uncover the new saloon version and the sports convertible.'	
4 'Now, team, this will be a major project so we thought we'd give you the background.'	
5 'In the next exercise, you can all practise the presentation skills we've talked about.'	
6 'This is the new accounting software I'm going to show you. Can you all see the screen?'	
7 'This is our new range of laptops. They will go on sale throughout Europe from August.'	

A press conference   B product launch   C workshop
D demonstration   E briefing   F lecture

59.2
8 marks

Choose the best word to fill each gap from the alternatives given below. Put a circle around the letter, A, B or C, of the word you choose.

'I am very worried about next week. I am doing a (1) .... presentation about our new advertising campaign. There will be about 30 people in the (2) .... – mainly regional sales managers. The (3) .... is a big hotel in London. They have excellent (4) .... so I don't have to worry about that. I've prepared the (5) .... of my talk but I'm still working on my visual (6) .... I've tried to (7) .... the main parts of my talk so I won't have to read from my notes. On Friday, I'm going to (8) .... the whole thing in front of a few friends from the department.'

1 A stand-up B sit-down C stand-down   5 A output B content C object
2 A viewing B crowd C audience   6 A helps B aids C supports
3 A position B venue C placing   7 A memories B memory C memorize
4 A facilities B faculties C functions   8 A rehearse B react C replay

59.3
4 marks

Write one word in the gap to complete each sentence. The first two or three letters are given.

1 I have planned the str...................... of my talk.
2 First I will in...................... myself.
3 Then I will out...................... what I'm going to talk about.
4 After I've given the presentation, I will invite people to ask qu...................... .

60.1
6 marks

Complete the 'Five Rules for Presenters' below. Use the notes to find the missing words. The first letters have been given.

Five Rules for Presenters	Notes
1 Start on time. Don't wait for l _ _ _ _ _ _ _ _ _.	Start on time. Don't wait for people who get to the presentation after the starting time.
2 Keep to the t _ _ _ _ _ _ in your plan.	Keep to the time that you have allocated to each point in your plan.
3 Don't l _ _ _ _ _ a particular point.	Don't go on and on about a particular point for a long time.
4 Don't d _ _ _ _ _ _.	Don't go off the point and talk about things that aren't in your plan.
5 Don't r _ _ o _ _ _ time.	Don't go on past the time when the presentation is supposed to finish.

60.2
8 marks

Choose the best word to fill each gap from the alternatives given below. Put a circle around the letter, A, B or C, of the word you choose.

'Here is some advice for making a presentation. People want to hear you, so (1) .... your voice to the back of the room. If you are using a (2) .... make sure you know how to turn it on. Speak in a natural (3) .... and not too quickly. Don't speak in a monotone – vary the (4) .... of your voice. Try to gain your audience's (5) .... from the beginning. Start with an interesting (6) .... In the main part of your talk, use some surprising (7) .... And don't forget to leave time for participants to ask (8) ....'

1 A shout	B project	C pass	5 A digression	B objective	C attention
2 A microphone	B microscope	C microlight	6 A anecdote	B antidote	C antelope
3 A tone	B sound	C note	7 A truths	B facts	C words
4 A court	B pitch	C field	8 A discussions	B practices	C questions

60.3
5 marks

The statements below were made in a presentation. Write one word in the gap to complete each statement.

1 'OK. To begin with, let's .... at what makes a good leader.'
2 'I'm digressing. Let's get .... to the point that Julie raised.'
3 'That's all I've got time .... now. We'll continue after lunch.'
4 'What does this mean in .... to leadership skills?'
5 'Now I'd like to .... to the issue of bullying at work.'

Your score
/19

Presentations 3: closing and questions

61.1
6 marks

The statements below were made by presenters responding to questions from the audience. Write one word in the gap to complete each statement.

1 'That's a fair p _ _ _ _. This model does assume that inflation is below 2%.'

2 'I can't tell you the bid price because that's c _ _ _ _ _ _ _ _ _ _ _ information.'

3 'That's not really my f _ _ _ _, but I think that my colleague Simon will be able to help you.'

4 'Ah. That really goes b _ _ _ _ _ the scope of this presentation. Perhaps we can talk afterwards?'

5 'I'm afraid we've run out of t _ _ _. We can return to that after lunch.'

6 'I'm sorry. I didn't c _ _ _ _ the question. Were you asking about stagflation?'

61.2
7 marks

Choose the best word to fill each gap from the alternatives given below. Put a circle around the letter, A, B or C, of the word you choose.

'OK. Let me (1) .... up what we've done today. (2) .... , we looked at what makes a good leader. (3) .... we looked at key leadership skills. Then, last, but by no means (4) .... , we talked about the consultation process. Are there any final (5) .... that you'd like to ask? No? Well then, that's a good (6) .... to stop. (7) .... you for listening.'

1	A run	B add	C sum
2	A Firstly	B Starting	C Openly
3	A Seconds	B Secondly	C Seconded
4	A last	B lost	C least
5	A questions	B answers	C information
6	A position	B place	C pointer
7	A Thank	B Thanks	C Thanking

61.3
5 marks

In each of the numbered sentences (1–5) there is *one* word which is *wrong*. Circle the mistake and write the correct word at the end of the line.

Here is some advice about making a presentation.

1 Remember to front the audience at all times. Don't turn your back on them. ....

2 Try to make eye contract with some of the participants as you speak. ....

3 Use jesters to stress key points but don't wave your hands around. ....

4 Control any manners you may have. They will distract the audience. ....

5 In my sight, the most important thing is to speak clearly. ....

Negotiations 1: situations and negotiators

62.1
5 marks

Draw a line from each word on the left to a word on the right to make a word pair. (There is one word that you don't have to use.) Then use your word pairs to complete the sentences below.

eleventh	chip
labour	dispute
bargaining	advantage
collective	solution
mutual	hour
	bargaining

1 This .... is getting worse and now seems likely to lead to a strike.
2 We think that this compromise is to our ....
3 Everyone is hoping that these .... discussions will be successful.
4 The high level of public support is a powerful .... for the firefighters.
5 I believe that .... is the right way to reach agreement about teachers' salaries.

62.2
7 marks

Decide which of the alternatives (A–E) each speaker is talking about. Write the letter of your answer in the box at the end of the sentence. You will have to use some alternatives more than once.

1 'We agree that when the new company is formed, there will be no forced redundancies.'	
2 'We've agreed to a rise of 2.5%, but the union also wants a minimum salary of £20,000.'	
3 'If the US taxes our steel exports, we will increase the tax on goods from the US.'	
4 'We start by asking for a very high price, then we negotiate down to a reasonable level.'	
5 'If we order 10,000 units from you, what discount will you offer us?'	
6 'The President of Energon will head the company and I have agreed to stay on as VP.'	
7 'The employers' offer is a joke. Our members deserve at least 8% this year.'	

A trade dispute   B merger negotiations   C customer–supplier negotiations
D wage negotiations   E bargaining tactic

62.3
5 marks

The statements below are about negotiations. Write one word in the gap to complete each statement. The first letter is given in each case.

1 'Rafi is a very tough n_ _ _ _ _ _ _ _ _ and always gets the best price.'
2 'These d_ _ _ _ _ _ _ negotiations could easily fail.'
3 'This p_ _ _ _ _ _ _ _ dispute has been going on for over two months now.'
4 'I'd say that the employers have all the bargaining p_ _ _ _ and will win in the end.'
5 'Last-m _ _ _ _ _ negotiations are going on to avoid an all-out strike.'

Your score
/17

Negotiations 2: preparing

63.1
5 marks

In each of the numbered sentences (1–5) there is *one* word which is *wrong*. Circle the mistake and write the correct word at the end of the line.

Good morning everyone. Perhaps we should start the meeting.

1 Welcome to our offices. I must admit that it is nice to be on home venue. ....

2 Our presentatives are Julia Gold and Sam Western. Oh, and me. ....

3 I think that we all know the foreground to these talks. ....

4 We've got a very tight tabletime today and a lot to discuss. ....

5 So, unless you have any questions, let's get out to business. ....

63.2
6 marks

Draw a line from each word on the left to a word on the right to make a word pair. (There is one word that you don't have to use.) Then use your word pairs to complete the sentences below.

kick	atmosphere
fallback	ground
neutral	priority
relaxed	talk
negotiating	off
small	position
	team

1 We will hold talks on .... so neither side has an advantage.

2 We'll .... the discussion by setting out our needs.

3 Our .... is very experienced and fully understands the process.

4 We believe the talks will be held in a .... with no real arguments.

5 We start with .... over coffee, but then it gets serious.

6 We have asked for 10%, but we do have a .... if that is turned down.

63.3
5 marks

Find the word that completes each tip on negotiating. The first and last letters of the answers are given.

1 Work out what you want to achieve: your ....

2 Decide on the most important things: your ....

3 Have a clear timetable for the talks: an ....

4 Don't waste time: get down to ....

5 Know the 'dos and don'ts' of negotiating: its ....

1	o							s
2	p							s
3	a				a			
4	b					s		
5	e						e	

64.1
5 marks

The statements below are about negotiations. Write one word in the gap to complete each statement.

1 'She asked a lot of p _ _ _ _ _ _ questions about the new contract.'
2 'We had to h _ _ _ _ _ over the price, but eventually got them for £20 each.'
3 'We'll pay $200 on c _ _ _ _ _ _ _ _ that you deliver by April 1st.'
4 'We will give you a 5% discount as l _ _ _ as you order more than 100 boxes.'
5 'We will c _ _ _ _ _ _ _ increasing our offer, provided you agree to call off the strike.'

64.2
6 marks

Choose the best word to fill each gap from the alternatives given below. Put a circle around the letter, A, B or C, of the word you choose.

'In a successful negotiation, no one should feel that they have lost. You should reach a win–
(1) .... solution. After one side makes a proposal, the other should make a (2) ....-offer.
If both sides make (3) .... you can work towards a compromise. By making a goodwill
(4) .... you may get something from the other side. It is this (5) ....-trading that moves
the negotiations along. If you are not prepared to make a (6) ....-off, there is a chance that
the talks will break down.'

1 A lose   B draw   C win
2 A counter   B condition   C consensus
3 A priorities B objectives   C concessions
4 A gesture   B mannerism   C etiquette
5 A bull   B horse   C bear
6 A business   B work   C trade

64.3
6 marks

Complete each sentence by writing in the gap a word formed from the verb given in brackets ( ).

1 We'll go back and think about your .... (propose)
2 If you take more than 1,000, we will consider .... you a discount. (give)
3 .... that this contract works out, we might offer you more work. (provide)
4 .... that you provide good service, we may agree to buy more cars. (suppose)
5 If you can finish the project by the end of the year, we could .... a bonus. (offer)
6 Good negotiators keep .... until they know what the other side really wants.
(probe)

Negotiations 4: difficulties

65.1
6 marks

Match each sentence beginning (1–6) with the correct ending. Write the letter (a–g) of the ending you choose in the box below. There is one extra ending that you don't have to use.

1	They threatened to sack us all but	a	confrontational right from the start.
2	Things are looking much better now	b	$240 is our final offer.
3	There is no point talking about it because	c	in the end we had to back down.
		d	we called their bluff and we're still in work.
4	We tried to stick to our demands but	e	have to be willing to compromise.
5	I'm afraid that the atmosphere was	f	our demand for 4% is non-negotiable.
6	We've looked at all the figures and	g	that we have found some common ground.

Answers 1 .... 2 .... 3 .... 4 .... 5 .... 6 ....

65.2
6 marks

The statements below are about difficult negotiations. Write one word in the gap to complete each statement.

1 'Having the public behind us gives us a lot of bargaining p.......................... .'
2 'The employers are negotiating from a position of s.......................... because unemployment is high.'
3 'They are making us negotiate under d.......................... . They are forcing us to accept their offer.'
4 'I'm pleased to tell you that the company has c.......................... down and accepted our demands.'
5 'The union has issued an u.......................... ; agree to everything or the workers strike.'
6 'We've made progress and there are only a few minor s.......................... points to resolve.'

65.3
5 marks

Clues 1–5 are about negotiating. Find the word that means the same as the clue. The first two or three letters of the answers are given.

1 Threaten to do something that you don't intend to do
2 Something that stands in the way of a solution
3 Reduce your demands
4 Make a trade-off to get something from the other side
5 Think about your position again

1	b	l					
2	o	b					
3	m	o	d				
4	c	o	m				
5	r	e					

66.1
10 marks

Choose the best word to fill each gap from the alternatives given below. Put a circle around the letter, A, B or C, of the word you choose.

There was bad news for the government today when negotiations between employers and the train drivers' union broke (1) .... A spokesperson for the union said that there was (2) .... 'The train owners are not prepared to compromise and so there is (3) ....' Barbara French of Northern Rail agreed that there were irreconcilable (4) .... and that the negotiators had reached an (5) .... The union has proposed that a (6) .... should be appointed to try to bring the two sides closer together. But (7) .... has been rejected by the employers, who wish to go straight to (8) .... This is unacceptable to the union which fears that an imposed (9) .... would not satisfy its members. This dispute is clearly far from (10) ....

1 A out	B in	C down	6 A negotiator	B director	C mediator
2 A deadlock	B dreadlock	C padlock	7 A discussion	B mediation	C confrontation
3 A checkmate	B stagnate	C stalemate	8 A arbitration	B arbitrate	C arbitrator
4 A sides	B differences	C bargains	9 A condition	B settlement	C decision
5 A impasse	B impassable	C impress	10 A answering	B finalize	C resolution

66.2
8 marks

Choose the best word from the brackets ( ) to fill the gap in each sentence.

1 I am very close to .... a deal with a key client.   (gripping/clinching/holding)
2 We have a .... contract with a new client in Singapore.   (voice/speaking/verbal)
3 She certainly drives a .... bargain, but we're happy with the result.
                                                    (hard/long/easy)
4 My .... contract says that I should get five weeks' holiday.
                                         (employment/position/situation)
5 This is a legally .... contract so you can't get out of it.   (fixing/holding/binding)
6 The only .... issue is the date of delivery.   (waiting/outstanding/lasting)
7 Can you draw .... a contract based on those points?   (out/up/in)
8 We've read your written .... and we think we can do business.
                                              (proposal/suggest/question)

66.3
5 marks

In each of the numbered sentences (1–5) there is *one* word which is *wrong*. Circle the mistake and write the correct word at the end of the line.

Well, I think we are close to a deal.
1 Let me just step over the main points that we've agreed.   ....
2 At price, we said $2 a unit for the first 10,000 units.   ....
3 As far as delivery is considered, we agreed the end of May.   ....
4 There's still the answer of storage to settle but that can wait.   ....
5 OK. I think that closes just about everything.   ....

Your score
/23

Summary Test 4

Read the questions carefully. Try to answer them all. This test takes about 45 minutes.

1
12 marks

For each sentence, choose the best word to fill the gap from the alternatives given.
Put a circle around the letter, A, B or C, of the word you choose.

1 I got your fax but the last page wasn't ....
   A reading   B legible   C written

2 Can you send me an e-mail with the data files .... ?
   A attached   B fixed   C linked

3 The directors have called an .... general meeting to discuss the debt crisis.
   A ordinary   B external   C extraordinary

4 Are there any issues arising from the .... of the last meeting?
   A hours   B minutes   C seconds

5 Let's go over the action .... agreed at last week's meeting.
   A points   B objectives   C tactics

6 I'm sorry, but increasing our bank loan is out of the ....
   A question   B opinion   C solution

7 If we don't find a .... , then our negotiations will break down.
   A position   B digression   C compromise

8 They announced the merger at a press .... last night.
   A workshop   B conference   C seminar

9 She is a good presenter, but she always runs .... time.
   A out   B over   C into

10 In my .... , we spend too much on corporate hospitality.
   A view   B thinking   C idea

11 They said it was their final offer but we .... their bluff.
   A conceded   B considered   C called

12 I'm pleased to say that we reached a .... late last night.
   A settlement   B mediation   C concession

2
6 marks

Match each sentence beginning (1–6) with the correct ending. Write the letter (a–g) of the ending you choose in the box below. There is one extra ending that you don't have to use.

1	If you give us a discount of 10%,	a	then we both need to make concessions.
2	This has been a very bitter dispute	b	we agreed on a reasonable price.
3	If we are going to break this deadlock,	c	with strong feelings on both sides.
4	I usually start with an anecdote	d	then we'll agree to buy 10,000 units.
5	You may be right there,	e	that covers just about everything.
6	Finally, after a lot of haggling,	f	but I'd need to see last month's figures.
		g	to gain the audience's attention.

Answers	1	2	3	4	5	6 ....

3

7 marks

Choose the best word from the box to complete each sentence. There is one extra word that you don't have to use.

down	up	over	under	in	out	on	off

1 I'll fax the drawings .... to you this afternoon.
2 I'm copying Richard and Ann .... on this e-mail.
3 Can we set .... a meeting for next Tuesday?
4 It was difficult to follow what Anil was saying because he kept wandering .... the point.
5 We said their demand was impossible to meet, but they wouldn't back ....
6 Can we move .... to the next point or are there any other questions?
7 The union is angry because it says it is being made to negotiate .... duress.

4

10 marks

Draw a line from each word on the left to a word on the right to make a word pair. (There is one extra word that you don't have to use.) Then use your word pairs to complete the sentences below. The first one is an example.

wage	aids
common	tactic
visual	contact
irreconcilable	negotiations
eleventh	ground
eye	hour
	differences

0 The ...._wage negotiations_........ between teachers' unions and their employers have broken down.
1 I've written the notes for my presentation, but I haven't prepared my
....
2 I try to make .... with members of the audience.
3 There are .... between the two sides in this dispute.
4 The mediator is looking for .... so he can propose a compromise.
5 We hope that these .... negotiations will break the stalemate.

5

8 marks

Complete the sentences below by writing one word in each gap. The first letter is given to help you.

1 A good chairperson will always listen to both s _ _ _ _ of the argument.
2 Will you be at the company's annual g _ _ _ _ _ _ meeting next week?
3 I circulated the a _ _ _ _ _ _ for the board meeting to all the directors.
4 In my o _ _ _ _ _ _ _, the new model is far too expensive.
5 This fax contains confidential i _ _ _ _ _ _ _ _ _ _.
6 The meeting was supposed to be today, but it has been p _ _ _ _ _ _ _ _ until Friday.
7 Asking people to work at the weekend is out of the q _ _ _ _ _ _ _.
8 We'll pay your asking price on c _ _ _ _ _ _ _ _ that you deliver by April.

In each sentence, there is *one* word which is *wrong*. Circle the mistake and write the correct word at the end of the line. The first one is an example.

0 I thought yesterday's seminar was very (producing.)   ...*productive*...
1 We covered a lot of groaned and I learnt a lot.   ....
2 I thought the group discusses were particularly useful.   ....
3 Tania chaired our group and really kept things moved along.   ....
4 People always want to regress and that wastes time.   ....
5 A few got quite excited but no one lost their temperature.   ....
6 I'm looking forward to the follow-up workplace next month.   ....

Match each headline to a statement. Write the number of the statement you choose in the box next to the headline. (There is one statement that you do not have to use.)

Companies crack down on staff e-mails ☐

Micropaq product launch delayed ☐

Europe to retaliate by taxing US imports ☐

Police pay talks enter difficult phase ☐

Goodwill gesture ends factory stoppage ☐

Teachers go to arbitration over pay ☐

1 A spokesperson said, 'We hope that this is not the start of a trade war.'
2 Both sides have agreed that they will accept the decision of the panel as binding.
3 The company said they would launch the new range in April – three months later than expected.
4 The delicate wage negotiations continue, with both sides careful about making trade-offs.
5 The company successfully negotiated a deal to supply 22 new aircraft over five years.
6 A survey showed that employees spend about 40 minutes a day sending messages to friends.
7 The union agreed to halt industrial action when the employers withdrew their ultimatum.

For each sentence, find *one* word to replace the underlined phrase. Write the word at the end of the sentence.

1 I'm also <u>sending a copy of</u> this e-mail to Ruth.   ....
2 When you give a talk, always check the <u>place where the presentation will be held</u>.   ....
3 We spent one hour <u>trying to produce as many ideas as possible</u>.   ....
4 The main <u>thing that we want to achieve</u> today is to set next month's sales targets.   ....
5 The talks finished in <u>a position where neither side would climb down</u>.   ....
6 We hope to find a <u>solution where both sides accept less than they wanted at first</u>.   ....

Choose the text (A–I) which best fits each gap in the e-mail below. There is one option that you do not have to use.

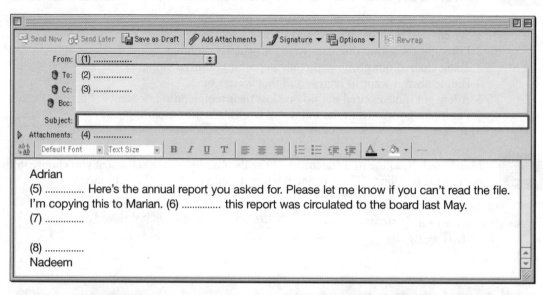

A Annual_Report_2003.doc
B Thanks for your e-mail.
C adrian.scott@edconsult.nl
D AFAIK
E N.Mohammed@inter4.org

F E-mail if you need anything else.
G Regards
H send and receive
I oakley.marian@group7.co.uk

Answers | 1 .... | 2 .... | 3 .... | 4 .... | 5 .... | 6 .... | 7 .... | 8 .... |

Match each statement (1–6) to one of the terms given below. Write the letter (A–H) in the box next to the statement. There are two terms that you don't have to use.

1 To sum up, I want to remind you of the four main points from today's seminar.	
2 I'm Ingrid Jensen and I shall be talking about quality assurance in the 21st century.	
3 Clearly, we all agree that something needs to be done to improve the canteen.	
4 If I can just stop you for a moment, Toni . . .	
5 I'm sorry, I seem to have wandered off the point.	
6 Speak slowly and clearly so that they can hear you at the back of the room.	

A digression   B conclusion   C interruption   D consensus
E gesture   F introduction   G mannerism   H voice projection

> This is the end of Summary Test 4.
> Use the Answer key at the back of the book to check your answers.

Answer key

How to use the Answer key

Give yourself one mark for a completely correct answer and zero for an incorrect answer. Add up all your marks to get your total score. Compare your total score with the 'target score' for the test.

Test 1 (Target = 16+)

1.1 (6 marks)
1 manage   2 of   3 under   4 responsibility
5 deal   6 responsible

1.2 (6 marks)
1 P   2 PT   3 T   4 FT   5 P   6 T

1.3 (6 marks)
for, to, get, at, off, of

1.4 (4 marks)
1 coordinating   2 make   3 design
4 planning

Test 2 (Target = 17+)

2.1 (6 marks)
human contact, problem solving, day shift, team work, clock on, working hours

2.2 (6 marks)
1 SW   2 TW   3 SW   4 OW
5 OW   6 TW

2.3 (6 marks)
1 flexitime   2 home   3 tiring
4 stimulating   5 clock   6 commuters

2.4 (6 marks)
1 hard   2 boring   3 routine   4 exciting
5 fascinating   6 tough

Test 3 (Target = 17+)

3.1 (4 marks)
employment agency, application form, curriculum vitae, psychometric test

3.2 (7 marks)
1 agency   2 positions   3 posts
4 application   5 shortlist   6 interview
7 appoint

3.3 (6 marks)
1 CL   2 CV   3 CL   4 SV   5 CV   6 SV

3.4 (6 marks)
1 qualifications   2 experience   3 headhunt
4 referees   5 selection   6 candidate

Test 4 (Target = 17+)

4.1 (6 marks)
from, in, as, with/at, in/at, for

4.2 (6 marks)
1 paper   2 work   3 training
4 development   5 motivated   6 player

4.3 (6 marks)
1 U   2 S-S   3 U   4 HS   5 U   6 HS *or* Sk

4.4 (6 marks)
1 proactive   2 methodical   3 numerate
4 talented   5 literate   6 self-driven

Test 5 (Target = 15+)

5.1 (7 marks)
1 earn   2 minimum   3 tips   4 salary
5 benefits   6 company   7 pension

5.2 (7 marks)
1 pay   2 overtime   3 perks
4 basic   5 commission   6 bonus   7 fringe

5.3 (6 marks)
1 H   2 B   3 E   4 A   5 D   6 F

Test 6 (Target = 15+)

6.1 (6 marks)
technical support, shop floor, open plan, head office, blue collar, workforce (*also* work plan)

6.2 (8 marks)
1 management   2 payroll   3 personnel
4 sites   5 manual   6 resources   7 staff
8 finance

6.3 (6 marks)
industrial, union, strike/stoppage, overtime, go-slow (2 marks)

Test 7 (Target = 17+)

7.1 (7 marks)
1 F   2 I   3 A   4 D   5 E   6 C   7 H

7.2 (10 marks)
1 resigned   2 off   3 path   4 reviews
5 leaner   6 senior   7 fired   8 temporary
9 job   10 dismissed

7.3 (7 marks)
flatter, redundant, retirement, demoted,
flexible, notice, outplacement

Test 8 (Target = 15+)

8.1 (6 marks)
1 E   2 B   3 D   4 A   5 C   6 D

8.2 (6 marks)
1 first   2 hazard   3 strain   4 passive
5 safety   6 environment

8.3 (8 marks)
1 bully (not *bull*)
2 harassment (not *harass*)
3 against (not *about*)
4 glass (not *wooden*)
5 sex/sexual (not *woman*)
6 opportunities (not *opportune*)
7 race/racial (not *racism*)
8 action (not *activation*)

Test 9 (Target = 14+)

9.1 (8 marks)
1 C   2 B   3 A   4 D   5 G   6 K
7 F   8 H

9.2 (6 marks)
1 up   2 line   3 boss   4 middle
5 VP   6 senior

9.3 (4 marks)
1 boardroom   2 president   3 Financial
4 Director

Test 10 (Target = 15+)

10.1 (6 marks)
1 founded   2 start-ups   3 captains
4 magnate   5 businesswoman   6 empire

10.2 (6 marks)
entrepreneur, establishing, grow, leadership,
tycoon, entrepreneurial

10.3 (7 marks – 1 for each word)
1 businessperson   2 movie mogul
3 founder   4 media   5 oil magnate

Test 11 (Target = 15+)

11.1 (6 marks)
corporate profits, self-employed, e-commerce,
free enterprise, enterprise zone, nationalized
industry

11.2 (6 marks)
1 B   2 C   3 A   4 C   5 B   6 A

11.3 (8 marks)
1 logo   2 disaster   3 multinational
4 enterprises   5 image   6 chamber
7 commerce   8 ladder

Test 12 (Target = 14+)

12.1 (6 marks)
1 self   2 society   3 public   4 sole
5 profit   6 fund

12.2 (6 marks)
1 A   2 C   3 A   4 C   5 A   6 B

12.3 (6 marks)
1 limited   2 company   3 freelancer
4 partnership   5 voluntary   6 donation

Test 13 (Target = 15+)

13.1 (7 marks)
B = telecommunications, C = pharmaceuticals,
D and F = aerospace, E = textiles, G = media,
H = construction

13.2 (6 marks)
1 tourism   2 healthcare   3 property
4 catering   5 leisure   6 financial services

13.3 (6 marks)
1 automobile   2 heavy   3 growth
4 software   5 goods   6 emerging

Test 14 (Target = 15+)

14.1 (8 marks)
1 B 2 A 3 C 4 C 5 A 6 B
7 A 8 C

14.2 (6 marks)
1 survey 2 consumer 3 scale 4 effective
5 trials 6 rollout

14.3 (6 marks)
1 concept 2 beta 3 CADCAM 4 defect
5 laboratory 6 recall

Test 15 (Target = 16+)

15.1 (6 marks)
1 designer 2 innovation 3 knowledge
4 inventor 5 developer 6 design/designs

15.2 (10 marks – 1 for each word pair and 1 for using the word pair in the correct sentence)
product development – sentence 2
cutting edge – sentence 3
research centre – sentence 5
under licence – sentence 1
intellectual property – sentence 4

15.3 (6 marks)
1 obsolete 2 art 3 technology 4 hi-tech
5 royalty 6 breakthrough

Test 16 (Target = 14+)

16.1 (6 marks)
1 produce 2 manufacturer 3 churn
4 line 5 shortage 6 Overcapacity

16.2 (6 marks)
1 B 2 C 3 A 4 A 5 C 6 B

16.3 (6 marks)
1 glut 2 robot 3 factory 4 assembly
5 workshop 6 hand-made

Summary Test 1 (Units 1–16)

1 (10 marks)
1 C 2 A 3 C 4 B 5 A 6 B 7 A
8 C 9 C 10 B

2 (10 marks)
Human, Information, Executive Officer,
Computer Design, Strain Injury, Public
Limited

3 (5 marks)
1 c 2 b 3 e 4 f 5 a

4 (5 marks)
Floor 3, Floor 7, Floor 4, Floor 6, Floor 2

5 (7 marks)
1 for 2 off/out 3 against 4 in 5 on
6 out 7 as

6 (8 marks)
1 share 2 car 3 trade 4 flexitime
5 estate 6 résumé 7 graduate
8 owner/proprietor

7 (10 marks – 1 for each word pair and 1 for using the word pair in the correct sentence)
sexual harassment – sentence 4
software tycoon – sentence 3
minimum wage – sentence 1
paper qualifications – sentence 2
night shift – sentence 5

8 (8 marks)
1 group 2 fault/defect 3 sector
4 forecast 5 property 6 capacity
7 vacant 8 employed

9 (6 marks – $\frac{1}{2}$ mark for finding the error and $\frac{1}{2}$ mark for writing the correct word)
1 privatized/privatised (not *privately*)
2 enterprise (not *entrepreneur*)
3 industry (not *industrial*)
4 intensive (not *expensive*)
5 edge (not *side*)
6 commercial (not *commerce*)

10 (6 marks)
Fat cats = 6, Demutualization = 1,
Enterprise Zone = 3, Jobs shock = 7,
Skills shortage = 2, Overtime ban = 4

Interpreting your score for Summary Test 1

60–75	Excellent – you are proficient in the use of the business vocabulary of Units 1–16.
54–59	Good – you are close to becoming proficient in the use of the business vocabulary of Units 1–16.
below 54	You are some way below the proficiency level. Go back and revise Units 1–16.

Test 17 (Target = 14+)

17.1 (5 marks)
1 B   2 A   3 A   4 C   5 B

17.2 (7 marks)
1 A   2 C   3 F   4 B   5 H   6 E   7 D

17.3 (6 marks)
1 handle   2 inputs   3 financed
4 outsource   5 efficiently   6 inventories

Test 18 (Target = 16+)

18.1 (10 marks – 1 for each word pair and 1 for using the word pair in the correct sentence)
quality control – sentence 3
mystery shoppers – sentence 1
zero defects – sentence 4
spot checks – sentence 5
best practice – sentence 2

18.2 (6 marks)
1 C   2 A   3 B   4 B   5 A   6 C

18.3 (6 marks – 1 for each word)
1 Total Quality Management
2 Business Process Re-engineering

Test 19 (Target = 16+)

19.1 (6 marks)
1 clientele   2 vendor   3 reforms   4 free
5 customers   6 users

19.2 (10 marks – 1 for each word pair and 1 for using the word pair in the correct sentence)
customer base – sentence 3
end users – sentence 2
street vendor – sentence 1
purchasing manager – sentence 5
market forces – sentence 4

19.3 (6 marks)
1 place   2 price   3 pressures   4 economy
5 client   6 consumers

Test 20 (Target = 14+)

20.1 (6 marks)
1 C   2 A   3 B   4 A   5 C   6 B

20.2 (6 marks)
1 growth   2 leader   3 share
4 segmentation   5 competition   6 player

20.3 (6 marks)
Across: 1 penetrate, 3 leave, 6 monopolize
Down: 2 rival, 4 fierce, 5 low

Test 21 (Target = 14+)

21.1 (6 marks)
1 C   2 B   3 A   4 C   5 B   6 A

21.2 (6 marks)
1 concept   2 benefits   3 oriented
4 packaging   5 marketer (*or* marketeer)
6 place

21.3 (6 marks)
1 mix   2 driven   3 features   4 promoting
5 benefits   6 led

Test 22 (Target = 14+)

22.1 (6 marks)
1 D   2 A   3 F   4 B   5 G   6 C

22.2 (6 marks)
1 portfolio   2 model   3 line   4 image
5 consumer   6 branding

22.3 (6 marks)
1 mix (not *mixture*)
2 range (not *ranger*)
3 identity (not *identify*)
4 positioning (not *depositing*)
5 own- (not *owner-*)
6 awareness (not *aware*)

Test 23 (Target = 15+)

23.1 (10 marks – 1 for each word pair and 1 for using the word pair in the correct sentence)

price cut – sentence 4
list price – sentence 3
up market – sentence 5
bottom end – sentence 1
entry level – sentence 2

23.2 (7 marks)
1 B 2 A 3 C 4 B 5 C 6 A 7 B

23.3 (5 marks)
1 boom 2 mid-priced 3 niche
4 mid-range 5 trade up

Test 24 (Target = 20+)

24.1 (8 marks)
1 G 2 H 3 E 4 I 5 D 6 F 7 A 8 B

24.2 (10 marks – 1 for each word pair and 1 for using the word pair in the correct sentence)

chain store – sentence 5
deep discounters – sentence 4
direct marketing – sentence 1
cold calls – sentence 3
call centre – sentence 2

24.3 (6 marks)
1 junk 2 outlet 3 middlemen
4 department 5 convenience
6 distributors

Test 25 (Target = 17+)

25.1 (6 marks)
1 advertising
2 advertisement *or* advert *or* ad
3 endorsement
4 sponsorship
5 promotion
6 competition

25.2 (10 marks – 1 for each word pair and 1 for using the word pair in the correct sentence)

sales territory – sentence 4
special offer – sentence 5
free samples – sentence 1
loyalty card – sentence 2
cross promotion – sentence 3

25.3 (6 marks)
1 medium 2 gift 3 sales force
4 campaign 5 sales 6 advertisers

Test 26 (Target = 20+)

26.1 (10 marks)
1 commerce 2 users 3 hits 4 engine
5 cart 6 securely 7 last 8 e-tailing
9 bricks 10 surfing

26.2 (6 marks)
1 service (not *serving*)
2 access (not *excess*)
3 account (not *accountant*)
4 name (not *word*)
5 password (not *passport*)
6 Wide (not *Wild*)

26.3 (9 marks)
B2C: business to consumer (*or* customer)
B2B: business to business
B2G: business to government

1 B2C 2 B2G 3 B2B 4 B2B 5 B2G
6 B2C

Test 27 (Target = 18+)

27.1 (8 marks)
1 on 2 sale 3 make 4 unit 5 target
6 direct 7 price 8 growth

27.2 (6 marks)
costing, production, overheads, total, mark, profit

27.3 (8 marks)
1 net 2 COGS 3 gross 4 volume
5 revenue 6 turnover 7 expenses
8 forecast

Test 28 (Target = 13+)

28.1 (5 marks)
1 profit 2 break 3 loss 4 money
5 profitable

28.2 (5 marks)
budget, spend *or* expenditure, expenditure *or* spend, overspent, over

28.3 (6 marks)
1 cash 2 for 3 point 4 leaders
5 economies 6 learning

Test 29 (Target = 15+)

29.1 (9 marks)
1 order 2 ship 3 billing 4 policy
5 flow 6 Inland 7 written 8 terms
9 receivable

29.2 (5 marks)
1 place (not *put*)
2 dispatched (not *displaced*)
3 credit (not *debit*)
4 owe (not *own*)
5 debts (not *depths*)

29.3 (6 marks)
1 key 2 debtors 3 creditors 4 discount
5 upfront 6 invoice *or* bill

Test 30 (Target = 13+)

30.1 (6 marks)
1 concern 2 Fixed 3 book 4 Current
5 intangible 6 goodwill

30.2 (5 marks)
1 depreciate 2 amortize 3 written
4 charge 5 balance

30.3 (5 marks)
1 liabilities 2 brands 3 off 4 financial
5 long-term

Test 31 (Target = 14+)

31.1 (8 marks)
1 C 2 A 3 C 4 C 5 B 6 A
7 B 8 B

31.2 (5 marks)
1 exceptional loss 2 accounting standards
3 bookkeeper 4 bottom line
5 window dressing

31.3 (5 marks)
1 accountant (not *accountancy*)
2 accounts (not *accounting*)
3 loss (not *lost*)
4 gross (not *growth*)
5 net (not *netting*)

Test 32 (Target = 18+)

32.1 (12 marks)
1 B 2 A 3 C 4 B 5 A 6 C
7 B 8 A 9 C 10 C 11 A 12 B

32.2 (5 marks)
1 G 2 D 3 H 4 E (*or* A) 5 A

32.3 (5 marks)
1 dividend 2 security 3 lender
4 gearing 5 borrowing

Summary Test 2 (Units 17–32)

1 (12 marks)
1 C 2 A 3 C 4 B 5 B 6 A 7 C
8 A 9 C 10 B 11 B 12 A

2 (6 marks)
1 e 2 a 3 f 4 g 5 b 6 c

3 (7 marks)
1 up 2 over 3 off 4 in 5 under
6 on 7 out

4 (10 marks – 1 for each word pair and 1 for using the word pair in the correct sentence)
best practice – sentence 2
shopping cart – sentence 5
customer base – sentence 4
product placement – sentence 1
convenience store – sentence 3

5 (8 marks)
1 materials 2 market 3 brand
4 medium 5 costs 6 assets 7 shoppers
8 account

6 (6 marks)
1 needs (not *wants*)
2 in (not *off*)
3 spot (not *spotting*)
4 wholesalers (not *holesalers*)
5 engine (not *machine*)
6 turnover (not *turnout*)

7 (6 marks)
Market leader = 3, Dividend fury = 5,
Price boom = 6, Franchise = 4,
E-tailer = 7, Move upmarket = 1

8 (8 marks)
Service Provider, Government, Goods Sold,
Moving Consumer, Process

9 (6 marks)
1 F 2 A 3 D 4 E 5 C 6 H

10 (6 marks)
1 marketing 2 catalogue/catalog 3 credit
4 auditors 5 discount 6 password

Interpreting your score for Summary Test 2

60–75	Excellent – you are proficient in the use of the business vocabulary of Units 17–32.
54–59	Good – you are close to becoming proficient in the use of the business vocabulary of Units 17–32.
below 54	You are some way below the proficiency level. Go back and revise Units 17–32.

Test 33 (Target = 14+)

33.1 (5 marks)
round *or* around, on, out, into, up

33.2 (6 marks)
1 B 2 A 3 C 4 C 5 B 6 A

33.3 (7 marks)
1 bankruptcy (not *bankruptness*)
2 creditors (not *credits*)
3 crisis (not *cries*)
4 reschedule (not *schedule*)
5 collapse (not *collide*)
6 trading (not *traiding*)
7 recovery (not *recover*)

Test 34 (Target = 15+)

34.1 (9 marks)
1 interest 2 holding 3 venture
4 friendly 5 pill 6 knight 7 parent
8 diversified 9 core

34.2 (5 marks)
1 prey (not *pray*)
2 hostile (not *hostage*)
3 acquire (not *ackquier*)
4 conglomerate (not *conglomerus*)
5 merger (not *murger*)

34.3 (6 marks)
1 unfocused 2 majority 3 divestment
4 alliance 5 acquisition 6 diversify

Test 35 (Target = 17+)

35.1 (6 marks)
1 B 2 G 3 A 4 D 5 C 6 F

35.2 (10 marks)
1 B 2 A 3 B 4 C 5 C 6 A 7 B
8 A 9 C 10 B

35.3 (5 marks)
1 unit 2 windfall 3 state 4 scheme
5 investors

Test 36 (Target = 14+)

36.1 (6 marks)
1 E 2 B 3 H 4 G 5 D 6 F

36.2 (6 marks)
1 financial 2 derivatives 3 dealers
4 flotation 5 speculator 6 securities

36.3 (6 marks)
1 B 2 A 3 C 4 A 5 C 6 B

Test 37 (Target = 15+)

37.1 (8 marks)
1 A 2 B 3 A 4 B 5 C 6 A
7 C 8 B

37.2 (6 marks)
1 turnover (not *turnoff*)
2 hands (not *arms*)
3 demand (not *demanding*)
4 gains (not *ganes*)
5 barrier (not *bar*)
6 market (not *index*)

37.3 (5 marks)
1 crash 2 price 3 index 4 panic
5 capitalization/capitalisation

Test 38 (Target = 14+)

38.1 (6 marks)
1 economy 2 indicators 3 domestic
4 surplus 5 rate 6 work

38.2 (5 marks)
1 financial 2 product 3 unemployment
4 inflationary 5 growth

38.3 (6 marks)
1 high 2 output 3 exports 4 jobless
5 inflation 6 economical

Test 39 (Target = 16+)

39.1 (8 marks)
1 D 2 A 3 C 4 E 5 B 6 A 7 D
8 C *or* E

39.2 (8 marks)
1 peaked 2 eased 3 off 4 slash
5 recession 6 Stagflation 7 axe
8 demand

39.3 (4 marks)
1 boom 2 negative 3 depression
4 trough

Test 40 (Target = 14+)

40.1 (6 marks)
1 C 2 G 3 A 4 D 5 E 6 B

40.2 (6 marks)
1 corruption 2 rigging 3 dealing
4 bribery 5 faking 6 forgery

40.3 (5 marks)
1 regulate (not *regular*)
2 wrongdoing (not *wrongdone*)
3 sweetener (not *sweetness*)
4 scam (not *scram*)
5 fraud (not *frawd*)

Test 41 (Target = 12+)

41.1 (9 marks)
1 B 2 C 3 A 4 A 5 B 6 C 7 C
8 A 9 B

41.2 (6 marks)
1 ethically 2 ethical 3 affirmative
4 discrimination 5 activists
6 environmental

Test 42 (Target = 14+)

42.1 (8 marks)
1 lead (not *leader*)
2 timeframe (not *frametime*)
3 schedule (not *scheduling*)
4 delay (not *delayment*)
5 downtime (not *uptime*)
6 behind (not *before*)
7 up (not *out*)
8 longer (not *long*)

42.2 (6 marks)
1 timetable *or* timeframe *or* timescale
2 stage *or* step
3 parallel
4 overlap
5 Completion
6 bonus

42.3 (5 marks)
1 calendar 2 organizer/organiser
3 prioritize/prioritise 4 distracted
5 quality

Test 43 (Target = 14+)

43.1 (6 marks)
1 rewarding 2 stimulating 3 challenging
4 stretched 5 overwhelmed 6 burnout

43.2 (6 marks)
1 under 2 induced 3 strains 4 nervous
5 race 6 treadmill

43.3 (6 marks)
1 out (not *outwards*)
2 overworked (not *overemployed*)
3 lifestyle (not *lifestyling*)
4 quality (not *qualification*)
5 downshifting (not *backshifting*)
6 unstressful (not *unstrainful*)

Test 44 (Target = 15+)

44.1 (10 marks)
1 C 2 A 3 D 4 B 5 D 6 A 7 D
8 C 9 A 10 B

44.2 (5 marks)
1 initiative 2 delegation 3 Empowerment
4 consensus 5 leadership

44.3 (4 marks)
1 flair 2 dynamism 3 charisma
4 visionary

Test 45 (Target = 15+)

45.1 (8 marks)
1 F 2 B 3 D 4 A 5 C 6 B
7 E 8 F

45.2 (5 marks)
1 making 2 layers *or* levels 3 equals
4 long 5 culture

45.3 (5 marks)
1 approachable (not *approachive*)
2 familiar (not *family*)
3 remote (not *remove*)
4 accessible (not *excessable*)
5 deference (not *difference*)

Test 46 (Target = 13+)

46.1 (6 marks)
1 C 2 A 3 C 4 B 5 A 6 B

46.2 (10 marks)
1 True 2 Does not say 3 True 4 False
5 Does not say 6 False 7 True
8 Howard 9 BSc and MBA 10 Caspar

Test 47 (Target = 14+)

47.1 (5 marks – $\frac{1}{2}$ for each word pair and $\frac{1}{2}$ for using the word pair in the correct sentence)
working breakfast – sentence 4
corporate hospitality – sentence 5
lunch break – sentence 2
public holiday – sentence 3
eye contact – sentence 1

47.2 (6 marks)
1 entertainment 2 punctuality 3 business
4 presenteeism 5 gestures 6 humour

47.3 (7 marks)
1 greeting (not *greet*)
2 contact (not *contract*)
3 presents (not *pressants*)
4 conversation (not *conversion*)
5 interrupt (not *enterrup*)
6 silence (not *silent*)
7 Goodbye (not *Good buying*)

Test 48 (Target = 22+)

48.1 (10 marks)
1 C 2 F 3 C 4 G 5 A 6 H 7 B
8 E 9 A 10 D

48.2 (9 marks)
1 call 2 cordless 3 pager 4 line 5 up
6 centre 7 toll 8 ring 9 card

48.3 (8 marks – 2 for each completely correct number and 1 for a number with *one* mistake)
01223 560499
0800 771177
44 181 3030
1800 555555

Test 49 (Target = 13+)

49.1 (17 marks – 1 for each word)
1 direct, voicemail, back
2 busy/engaged, hang
3 extension/number, switchboard, operator
4 through, wrong
5 cut, busy/engaged
6 dial *or* press, dialling
7 keypad
8 return, back/you/again

Test 50 (Target = 11+)

50.1 (9 marks)
Conversation 1: speak, afraid, leave, back
Conversation 2: Speaking, good, later
Conversation 3: take, about

50.2 (5 marks)
Hermann, thompson-clarke@aol.com,
van Lent, BA 471, www.art.house.org/music

Test 51 (Target = 16+)

51.1 (11 marks)
Conversation 1: fix, check *or* consult, about,
to, make, say, forward
Conversation 2: suitable, able, fine, calling

51.2 (11 marks)
Message 1: make, up, Would, put, touch
Message 2: possible, got, back, snowed, open,
soon

Summary Test 3 (Units 33–51)

1 (12 marks)
1 C   2 A   3 B   4 B   5 C   6 A   7 A
8 C   9 B   10 C   11 A   12 C

2 (6 marks)
1 d   2 f   3 b   4 c   5 a   6 g

3 (7 marks)
1 out   2 in   3 off   4 on   5 up   6 behind
7 under

4 (10 marks – 1 for each word pair and 1 for using the word pair in the correct sentence)
macho culture – sentence 4
direct line – sentence 3
nervous breakdown – sentence 1
smart casual – sentence 5
public holiday – sentence 2

5 (8 marks)
1 rate   2 account   3 chips   4 tone
5 dealing   6 venture   7 approach
8 contact

6 (6 marks)
1 initiative (not *initiate*)
2 empower (not *power*)
3 stimulated (not *simulated*)
4 code (not *note*)
5 discrimination (not *decrimination*)
6 soared (not *sawed*)

7 (6 marks)
Top executives = 6, Dress-down = 2,
Mobiles report = 7, Green investors = 5,
Sweatshop claim = 1, CEO's backhander = 3

8 (8 marks)
1 A   2 C   3 D   4 B   5 A   6 D
7 E   8 B

9 (6 marks)
1 H   2 B   3 G   4 E   5 C   6 A

10 (6 marks)
1 recession   2 dealer *or* trader
3 unemployment   4 counterfeit
5 timeframe/timetable/timescale
6 consultation

Interpreting your score for Summary Test 3

60–75	Excellent – you are proficient in the use of the business vocabulary of Units 33–51.
54–59	Good – you are close to becoming proficient in the use of the business vocabulary of Units 33–51.
below 54	You are some way below the proficiency level. Go back and revise Units 33–51.

Test 52 (Target = 14+)

52.1 (9 marks)
Conversation 1: send, number, me, fax
Conversation 2: get, legible, resend
Conversation 3: jammed, through

52.2 (8 marks: 1 for each word)
1 cover sheet   2 confidential information
3 intended recipient   4 advise   sender

Test 53 (Target = 12+)

53.1 (6 marks)
1 B   2 C   3 D (*or* E *or* G)   4 F   5 H   6 E

53.2 (8 marks)
1 four (4)
2 No (1 mark) because he sent it as a blind copy or 'Bcc' (1 mark)
3 for (not *about*), attached (not *attaching*), read (not *legible*), copying (not *copy*), regards *or* wishes (not *regard*)

Test 54 (Target = 18+)

54.1 (8 marks)
1 set   2 forward   3 postponed   4 chair
5 attend   6 miss   7 with   8 chat

54.2 (8 marks)
1 E   2 B   3 D   4 C   5 A   6 C   7 D
8 E

54.3 (6 marks)
1 time (not *timing*)
2 discussions (not *discusses*)
3 moving (not *move*)
4 ramble (not *scramble*)
5 ground (not *earth*)
6 productive (not *producing*)

Test 55 (Target = 16+)

55.1 (6 marks)
1 B 2 C 3 A 4 B 5 C 6 A

55.2 (8 marks)
1 take 2 record 3 matters 4 action
5 allocated 6 point 7 resolved 8 move

55.3 (5 marks)
1 agenda 2 timetable 3 tactfully
4 latecomer 5 digression

Test 56 (Target = 16+)

56.1 (7 marks)
1 A 2 C 3 B 4 A 5 B 6 C 7 B

56.2 (6 marks)
1 discussion (not *discuss*)
2 know (not *knowing*)
3 opinion (not *opinions*)
4 believe (not *belief*)
5 course (not *coarse*)
6 views (not *reviews*)

56.3 (6 marks)
1 business 2 objective 3 arranged
4 feelings 5 clear 6 Obviously

Test 57 (Target = 14+)

57.1 (10 marks)
1 A 2 C 3 B 4 B 5 A 6 C 7 A
8 C 9 B 10 C

57.2 (7 marks – $\frac{1}{2}$ for the word and $\frac{1}{2}$ for the classification of each sentence)
1 perfectly (SA) 2 question (SD)
3 agree (SA) 4 suppose (MA)
5 absurd (SD) 6 along (MD) 7 right (MA)

Test 58 (Target = 17+)

58.1 (7 marks)
1 point 2 mean 3 coming 4 interrupt
5 earlier 6 understand
7 suggesting *or* saying

58.2 (10 marks)
1 B 2 A 3 C 4 C 5 B 6 C 7 A
8 A 9 B 10 C

58.3 (6 marks)
1 C 2 I 3 H 4 C 5 H 6 I

Test 59 (Target = 16+)

59.1 (7 marks)
1 F 2 A 3 B 4 E 5 C 6 D 7 B

59.2 (8 marks)
1 A 2 C 3 B 4 A 5 B 6 B 7 C
8 A

59.3 (4 marks)
1 structure 2 introduce 3 outline
4 questions

Test 60 (Target = 15+)

60.1 (6 marks – 1 for each word)
1 latecomers 2 timings 3 labour
4 digress 5 run (1 mark) over (1 mark)

60.2 (8 marks)
1 B 2 A 3 A 4 B 5 C 6 A
7 B 8 C

60.3 (5 marks)
1 look 2 back 3 for 4 relation 5 turn

Test 61 (Target = 14+)

61.1 (6 marks)
1 point 2 confidential 3 field 4 beyond
5 time 6 catch

61.2 (7 marks)
1 C 2 A 3 B 4 C 5 A 6 B 7 A

61.3 (5 marks)
1 face (not *front*)
2 contact (not *contract*)
3 gestures (not *jesters*)
4 mannerisms (not *manners*)
5 view *or* opinion (not *sight*)

Test 62 (Target = 13+)

62.1 (5 marks – $\frac{1}{2}$ for the word pair and $\frac{1}{2}$ for the sentence)
eleventh-hour – sentence 3
labour dispute – sentence 1
bargaining chip – sentence 4
collective bargaining – sentence 5
mutual advantage – sentence 2

62.2 (7 marks)
1 B 2 D 3 A 4 E 5 C 6 B 7 D

62.3 (5 marks)
1 negotiator 2 delicate 3 prolonged
4 power 5 minute

Test 63 (Target = 13+)

63.1 (5 marks)
1 ground (not *venue*)
2 representatives (not *presentatives*)
3 background (not *foreground*)
4 timetable (not *tabletime*)
5 down (not *out*)

63.2 (6 marks – ½ for the word pair and ½ for the sentence)
kick off – sentence 2
fallback position – sentence 6
neutral ground – sentence 1
relaxed atmosphere – sentence 4
negotiating team – sentence 3
small talk – sentence 5

63.3 (5 marks)
1 objectives   2 priorities   3 agenda
4 business   5 etiquette

Test 64 (Target = 13+)

64.1 (5 marks)
1 probing   2 haggle   3 condition   4 long
5 consider

64.2 (6 marks)
1 C   2 A   3 C   4 A   5 B   6 C

64.3 (6 marks)
1 proposal   2 giving   3 Provided/Providing
4 Supposing   5 offer   6 probing

Test 65 (Target = 13+)

65.1 (6 marks)
1 d   2 g   3 f   4 c   5 a   6 b

65.2 (6 marks)
1 power   2 strength   3 duress   4 climbed
5 ultimatum   6 sticking

65.3 (5 marks)
1 bluff   2 obstacle   3 moderate
4 compromise   5 reconsider

Test 66 (Target = 17+)

66.1 (10 marks)
1 C   2 A   3 C   4 B   5 A   6 C   7 B
8 A   9 B   10 C

66.2 (8 marks)
1 clinching   2 verbal   3 hard
4 employment   5 binding   6 outstanding
7 up   8 proposal

66.3 (5 marks)
1 run *or* go (not *step*)
2 On (not *At*)
3 concerned (not *considered*)
4 question (not *answer*)
5 covers (not *closes*)

Summary Test 4 (Units 52–66)

1 (12 marks)
1 B   2 A   3 C   4 B   5 A   6 A   7 C
8 B   9 B   10 A   11 C   12 A

2 (6 marks)
1 d   2 c   3 a   4 g   5 f   6 b

3 (7 marks)
1 over   2 in   3 up   4 off   5 down
6 on   7 under

4 (10 marks – 1 for each word pair and 1 for using the word pair in the correct sentence)
common ground – sentence 4
visual aids – sentence 1
irreconcilable differences – sentence 3
eleventh-hour – sentence 5
eye contact – sentence 2

5 (8 marks)
1 sides   2 general   3 agenda   4 opinion
5 information   6 postponed   7 question
8 condition

6 (6 marks)
1 ground (not *groaned*)
2 discussions (not *discusses*)
3 moving (not *moved*)
4 digress (not *regress*)
5 temper (not *temperature*)
6 workshop (not *workplace*)

7 (6 marks)
Staff e-mails = 6, Product launch = 3,
Europe to retaliate = 1, Police pay = 4,
Goodwill gesture = 7, Teachers' pay = 2

8 (6 marks)
1 copying   2 venue   3 brainstorming
4 objective/purpose/aim
5 deadlock/stalemate
6 compromise

9 (8 marks)
1 E   2 C   3 I   4 A   5 B   6 D
7 F   8 G

10 (6 marks)
1 B   2 F   3 D   4 C   5 A   6 H

Interpreting your score for Summary Test 4

60–75	Excellent – you are proficient in the use of the business vocabulary of Units 52–66.
54–59	Good – you are close to becoming proficient in the use of the business vocabulary of Units 52–66.
below 54	You are some way below the proficiency level. Go back and revise Units 52–66.

Acknowledgements

The authors and publishers would like to thank the following schools and individuals who pre-tested and reviewed this material:

Tim Banks, The British Council, Czech Republic; Tracey J. Innes, Advanced Corporate Training, Poland; Helena Sharman, Linguarama, UK; Cameron Slater, Linguarama Business Language School, UK; George Tomaszewski, Transfer Conseil Formation, France; Julian Wheatley, Freelance, Germany.

We are also grateful to Alison Silver for her editorial work and Karen Donnelly and Martin Aston for the illustrations.

Design, production and page layout by Kamae Design, Oxford.